PRAISE FOR
IN HIS HANDS

Vonette Bright is a grandmother of the faith from whom we can all draw strength, guidance and perspective. In her genuine and down to earth fashion, she shares how difficult seasons can position every woman to realize the significance of her faith and influence in her world. *In His Hands* will open your heart and eyes to see your potential as a faith-filled world changer and set you on the course of an overflowing walk with God!

Lisa Bevere
Bestselling Author and Speaker, Messenger International

Vonette Bright is one who has walked well through a dark hour and true test of faith. In this book, she shares how faith, like a precious gem, is made beautiful over time and through a process. She uses her experience to encourage women of all ages to embrace their own journey and see the significance of faith walked out on a daily basis. *In His Hands* will show you how to find purpose and develop strong faith for the different seasons of life.

Christine Caine
Director of Equip and Empower Ministries
Founder of the A21 Campaign

I have come to know Vonette Bright as a co-author, friend and a mentor. Her faith is an inspiration, the power of her prayers is a blessing, and the love she has for our Lord is a shining example of a life surrendered to Him. She is a woman to listen to, to admire and to emulate.

Nancy Moser
Bestselling Fiction Author, *Masquerade* and *Mozart's Sister*
Co-author of *The Sister Circle* series with Vonette Bright

After reading *In His Hands*, I feel like I have just been in the presence of a legend of faith. Her practical and stirring portrayal of a faith that lasts and can work miracles is something everyone needs to read. Psalm 145:4 tells us, "One generation shall praise Your works to another, and shall declare Your mighty acts" (*NASB*). Vonette has done that. She has written a magnificent book that generations following her can be inspired by and learn from. If your faith is strong, if your faith has grown weak, or if your faith needs a boost—please get this book. And then get one for a friend!

Holly Wagner

Author of *GodChicks, Daily Steps for GodChicks,* and *GodChicks and the Men They Love*

VONETTE BRIGHT

CO-FOUNDER, CAMPUS CRUSADE FOR CHRIST

In His Hands

Finding a Faith that Will Sustain You,
Encourage You and Give You Hope

Regal

From Gospel Light
Ventura, California, U.S.A.

Published by Regal
From Gospel Light
Ventura, California, U.S.A.
www.regalbooks.com
Printed in the U.S.A.

Library of Congress Cataloging-in-Publication Data
Bright, Vonette Z.
In His hands : finding a faith that will sustain you, encourage you, and give you hope /
Vonette Bright.
p. cm.
ISBN 978-0-8307-5497-7 (hard cover)
1. Christian women—Religious life. 2. Faith. I. Title.
BV4527.B7155 2010
248.8'43—dc22
2010013045

1 2 3 4 5 6 7 8 9 10 11 12 13 14 15 / 20 19 18 17 16 15 14 13 12 11 10

Rights for publishing this book outside the U.S.A. or in non-English languages are
administered by Gospel Light Worldwide, an international not-for-profit ministry.
For additional information, please visit www.glww.org, email info@glww.org, or write to
Gospel Light Worldwide, 1957 Eastman Avenue, Ventura, CA 93003, U.S.A.

To order copies of this book and other Regal products in bulk quantities,
please contact us at 1-800-446-7735.

To the CCCI staff

Contents

Vonette Bright's definition of faith:

Believing in that which is humanly impossible apart from a supernatural work of God.

FOREWORD

When the apostle Paul wanted people to understand the validity of his ministry, he pointed to the lives of those who "became imitators of us" so that "in every place your faith towards God has gone forth, so that we have no need to say anything" (1 Thess. 1:6,8, *NASB*).

For those who have "experienced" Vonette and Bill Bright and their day-to-day, moment-by-moment outliving of Christ, there is no need for the foreword; like Paul, I "have no need to say anything."

For those who have not been enriched by this experience, let me say that I have watched this precious couple seek to live by every word that comes from the mouth of God. Truly my beloved friend is an imitator of Christ, which is why I welcome every opportunity to learn everything I can from her.

I am honored by the privilege of writing a foreword to Vonette's book. Like me, you are going to learn much from a woman whose faith has been seasoned with time and experience, and broadened and deepened by the trials of life and by her associations with others from all strata across the nations.

I'm excited to know this book is in your hand. I have no doubt it will be used by our Father to polish the many facets of your faith through its precepts for life, its practical applications and its faith-building stories.

You'll find it a delightful and easy read and will come away encouraged to grow in the grace and knowledge of our Lord and Savior Jesus Christ—where "faith comes by hearing, and hearing by the word of Christ" (Rom. 10:17, *NASB*).

Kay Arthur
Author and CEO
Precept Ministries International

INTRODUCTION

Footprints of Faith

Remember your leaders who first taught you the word of God. Think of all the good that has come from their lives, and trust the Lord as they do.

HEBREWS 13:7

The familiar story of a father and his young son on a mountain-climbing expedition thrilled my heart when I first heard it; however it now takes on new meaning. The father was concerned about the safety of his son and watched him carefully as they scaled the mountainside. He called out to his son at one point to instruct with words of caution, to which the son replied, "I'm okay, Daddy. I'm putting my feet right in your footprints."

What wonderful confidence! There are few people whose steps I would want to follow consistently; however, there is one couple—Dr. and Mrs. Bill Bright—whose influence forever changed my life and encouraged my walk with Christ.

When we read articles about people who accomplish great things for Christ, our reactions range from wonder and awe and, sometimes, great motivation to strengthen our faith. It has been a privilege to spend precious time with Bill and Vonette Bright, staying in their home, observing closely two people who demonstrate truly authentic faith.

I feel that it is so important to tell you some of my observations because we are influenced by marketing gurus and publicity writers whose claims about products and people fall far short of reality. Well, the Master and Creator of all manufacturers and of all humankind gave the best instructions on how to test the validity of marketing claims. We can judge anything by the evidence. Yes, even fellow believers. We are instructed to judge believers only by the fruit they bear. We are to test the spirits. Remember, we will know they are Christians by their love.

Vonette has commented that their lives have been greatly influenced by the fact of being on public display most of the time and by a sincere desire to walk the walk, not just talk the talk. Since the early days of Campus Crusade for Christ, Bill and Vonette either lived with someone or had someone living with them. It is just pure fun to hear the stories of young people who have lived with them and served them in many different capacities.

In recent years, I have observed the teaching and mentoring that takes place as young women work in the office or in the home with Vonette, and also the dear young men who assisted Dr. Bright through days of physical limitations. Practical, victorious, genuine faith is the only way I can describe what I observed as they daily practiced what they preached and taught others to do the same.

Bill and Vonette Bright have been honored on many occasions, and I have read and heard many of the accolades offered them. Deserving as they were of the honors bestowed, I wish everyone could know the true depth of faith that was lived out by Bill, and that Vonette continues to demonstrate.

James 2:17 says it clearly: "So you see, it isn't enough just to have faith. Faith that doesn't show itself by good deeds is no faith at all—it is dead and useless."

A person's works truly reveal the authenticity of his or her faith. Bill and Vonette are wonderful examples of authentic faith. Their passion to know God and communicate His love to others has been the dominant force in their lives.

If I could take you on a walk through the hallways of the founder's office at Campus Crusade for Christ headquarters in Orlando, Florida, I wonder how long it would take for you to share my conclusion. From the earliest days of ministry, most of the photos capture moments with Bill and Vonette—together. At special times of recognition or social settings with high-profile people, there they were, side by side—two people with one passion to reach the world for Christ.

Companies pay great amounts of money to have celebrities endorse their products. We place confidence in a product because a recognizable voice or face has told us the product is valid. If you need an endorsement for your walk of faith, please accept my words about the evidence I have witnessed in the lives of Bill and Vonette Bright as the only way to live in this world and look joyfully toward an eternal life.

Vonette Bright is a beautiful and gracious woman to all who know her; however, the beliefs she expresses in this book are where the real beauty and strength shine forth. Her love for God's Word, her passion for people to know Christ, her consistency in prayer and her devotion to her husband have painted a picture on my soul that reflects the faith I desire in my life.

What you read in these pages will help you identify areas of your life that can be strengthened by developing a more authentic faith.

Brenda Josee

Looking Within

Understanding the reason why people buy certain products has become a topic of intense research and study. Why you buy a book keeps publishers speculating and authors writing. When you think of the volumes written on any given subject, you quickly realize you can't read them all. There must be some specific motivation to buy a book.

I wrote an earlier book titled *The Woman Within,* and it is in that book that I encouraged women to seriously recognize their potential and accept the indwelling of the Holy Spirit and walk in the awareness of His presence.

Now it is time to move beyond the introspection, and with a sense of urgency, I want every woman to develop an authentic faith and recognize that she is a potential world changer.

Believing in Jesus and being filled with the Spirit must not be simply a belief system; it must be more! What we believe becomes authentic when we live a life of faith—sharing, giving and serving.

There is a beautiful song with the lyrics "You're the only Jesus some will ever see." It is so important that the Jesus people see in you is genuine. I will move to the discussion of openly sharing your faith, but in the first chapters of this book, I want you to discover the amazing ability you have to demonstrate a credible faith that instills self-confidence and empowers you to love and care for others.

Attempting to communicate the concept of faith is daunting. Just think of an infant child trying to understand the concept of muscle development and motor skills; and yet with patience and guidance a child learns to walk, run, skip and hop. I am not certain we mere mortals can ever truly understand the concept of faith, but we can learn to live by faith when we realize that our faith is in a Person. The person of Jesus Christ provides us a source of confidence that guides our life and anchors our faith.

Too many people find all their confidence in knowledge, and yet our finite minds can never understand the true depth of faith. It seems the more we know about faith the less we understand. I can write to you today with a different level of confidence in my faith than was possible a few months ago. My faith sustained me through days and nights of the declining health of my husband while we were in the process of passing the mantle of leadership of Campus Crusade for Christ on to the next generation. I can tell you with confidence that when your faith is placed totally in Christ, and Christ alone, you find purpose in every moment on this earth and look excitedly toward the fulfillment of your faith for all eternity.

Dear brothers and sisters, whenever trouble comes your way, let it be an opportunity for joy. For when your faith is tested, your endurance has a chance to grow. So let it grow, for when your endurance is fully developed, you will be strong in character and ready for anything (Jas. 1:2-4).

For such a time as this,
Vonette Bright

1

The Value of Our Faith

*Faith is the whole man rightly related to God by the
power of the Spirit of Jesus Christ.*

OSWALD CHAMBERS

Every day we face challenges—some are minor and require little
thought about just what to do. Some challenges surprise us, and
some seem to be ongoing. You have probably read one of the scales
that attempt to rate various events in life and attach a point value
to the degree of trauma. When you are the one in the midst of a
challenge, point systems mean very little.

Fortunately, I am not of the type to borrow trouble or live anx-
iously in a "what-if" or "when" state of mind. My faith in Christ
has truly found a resting place, and when faced with the reality
that, barring a divine miracle of God, my husband would not live
much longer, the true test of my faith began to unfold. My partner in life, Bill Bright, was going to leave this earth, and my life
would most certainly change forever.

I was blessed to be Bill's wife. We loved and served together for
more than 50 years. We experienced adventure, challenge, a calling
from God, the joy of family and the intimacy of sharing our souls
with each other. The central purpose of our life was the same: to
worship and serve God. I couldn't have asked for a more satisfying
life. Now I was to face life and ministry without him.

The trauma began some years ago when Bill was diagnosed with
pulmonary fibrosis, an incurable disease that slowly incapacitates
the lungs. It was devastating news. My husband had always been a
tireless, energetic man who could keep on going longer than most
men half his age. With his heart to see the gospel of Jesus Christ

spread around the world, he traveled millions of miles per year, spoke thousands of times, attended countless meetings and, most of all, shared his faith in Christ with others everywhere he went. What would a debilitating disease do to him? Would it change his faith in God?

And what about me? We all "know" that we're mortal humans, yet that knowledge doesn't seem to penetrate to our core until we're faced with the surety of our own death. My entire Christian walk was built upon a faith in Jesus Christ and that I will see Him face to face one day. Would my faith withstand the pressure of this test?

I can tell you right now that not only did my faith withstand, but also it was the very foundation for the joy and steadfastness I experienced in the midst of the pain and sorrow. I saw so much more clearly that faith in Jesus Christ is the only answer to life's difficulties. I assure you that developing an authentic faith is the most important journey we take as women of God. In this book, I want to share with you the importance and the joys of living every moment of your life by faith in our wonderful Lord Jesus Christ. This can make your life's journey an overflowing walk with God.

The Joy of Faith

The word "faith" is tossed about quite casually today. We have "faith in our fellow man," "faith for the journey," "faith in myself." All these are generalities that don't mean much unless we can identify just what we mean by "faith." Is it just a vague belief? Is it positive thinking? Is it a good feeling about something?

How are any of us able to survive an unpredictable life? How do we remain at peace in a world where everything can change in a moment? If we are honest with ourselves, we will admit that we can't do it alone. Our human strength is too weak. Our tendency is to be anxious and insecure. But we can find security and peace. The great reformer, Martin Luther, embraced a verse that answers these questions: "The just shall live by faith" (Rom. 1:17, *KJV*). It's that simple. We must choose to walk by faith in God. That was my husband's goal: to live every moment by faith. Bill believed that our faith in Christ is the most essential part of our lives. I adopted it as my own objective too. This focus dramatically affected how we faced Bill's last days.

Early in 2003, Bill's condition began to deteriorate. We prayed for miracles to stem or heal the process of the illness, and we saw some supernatural answers to our prayers, but we also realized that God's will is not always what we desire at first. We sincerely wanted God's will to be done—even if that meant Bill would lose his battle with pulmonary fibrosis. By July, Bill had difficulty making himself understood when he spoke. I knew this meant the beginning of the end. I was going to have to face my partner's passing.

After that, Bill's condition began to deteriorate rapidly. On Saturday, July 12, he had trouble dictating his last project, called "A Charge to Staff." This was a challenge to Campus Crusade for Christ staff members who were meeting in Fort Collins, Colorado, for the biannual staff training conference. The plan had been for Bill to address the conference via video link, but even that was impossible now. As founder of Campus Crusade for Christ, his heart was to be with the staff, but he was too ill. In fact, that day he signed his last letters.

Dear ones, have you ever stood by as someone you love suffered? Perhaps it was an elderly parent or a child or, as it was for me, your spouse. There is no way to describe how a person's heart aches during a time like this. So many times, I wished I could take Bill's pain and discomfort on myself.

As Bill's condition worsened, he didn't want me to be away from his side. On Wednesday, he had a brief meeting with Mel Gibson, who was preparing to release his movie *The Passion of the Christ*. By God's grace, Bill was somewhat alert, but by the next day, he could no longer communicate. The man I had relied upon for so much could no longer speak words of love to me.

I was living a true test of my faith. There is no way I can explain to you why God would allow such a difficult disease to grip my husband. But one thing I can say with confidence—it was at this time that Bill's faith shone through most clearly. He truly trusted God in everything.

As he lay in the bed that day, I thought back to one point a few weeks earlier when his condition had taken a downward turn and he could still communicate clearly. I asked him, "Why do you think you're suffering? Why would God put you through this?"

Immediately, Bill replied, "I'm not suffering! It depends on the definition of suffering. Even gasping for breath for extended periods of time does not compare with what Christ went through during His trial and crucifixion. For Jesus, the agony of the trial was totally illegal. He was beaten beyond recognition; He had six hours of suffocating on the cross; He bore the sins of the world; He was cut off from God because of our sins, for there was no other way for man to be redeemed."

After catching his breath, Bill continued, "Then think about Peter being crucified head downward, Paul's persecution and, finally, his beheading. All the disciples were persecuted and finally martyred, except for John, who was exiled. Through the centuries, there have been many martyrs, so what I'm going through is very minor."

Then Bill began to pray, "Oh Father, how great You are!" Bill was continually filled with a spirit of praise.

You can't imagine what Bill's words and attitude meant to me. He reminded me that God is greater than any incident in our lives—no matter how difficult or painful. He gives us the purest joy in the midst of trials, and I experienced it all at that moment. I realized that my faith is my most precious possession. It was the only reason I could have joy in the midst of my sorrow.

By now, you may be wondering, *Just what is "faith" anyway? I've heard that word so many times, but it seems as elusive as a rainbow.* Understanding just what faith is and what it does for us will bring us a depth of knowledge about God and our relationship to Him.

What Is Faith?

I have heard many unbelievers say things like: "People who have faith are just believing in something even when the facts are against them." Or "Faith is an irrational belief in something that can never be proven true." What about this one? "Faith is just for those who are too weak to handle life."

It's true that many kinds of faith in this world are irrational ways of thinking. Do you remember hearing about the Heaven's Gate cult in the news a few years ago? The members all committed suicide for a belief they thought was real. People can also use faith as a term meaning some hazy or all-encompassing belief that doesn't really have any firmness attached to it. An example is the statement: "I have faith in the goodness of man." That belief doesn't help much if you're traveling in the wilds of Pakistan or get caught between warring factions in Indonesia.

These ideas about faith all misrepresent the faith that I have lived by for five decades. Did you know that the Bible defines faith for us? Hebrews 11:1 says, "What is faith? It is the confident assurance that what we hope for is going to happen. It is the evidence of things we cannot see." If you notice, the verse says that faith is "the *evidence* of things we cannot see." Our faith is not built on something so mysterious that all we can do is accept it blindly. God has given us a rational, justifiable, logical faith that makes sense.

What are the proofs of our faith—that God exists and that He sent His Son to die for us? This book's purpose is not to prove the existence of God, but let me give you a few examples of how God has given us proofs of His existence:

- The intricate and beautiful design of creation shows the nature of our God.
- The historical record of the Gospels proves the existence of Jesus.
- The growth of the Christian church proves the message of the Holy Spirit's work in this world.
- The change in a new believer proves the truth of the new birth.[1]

Our faith is steady and sure because it is built on the right foundation. Otherwise, our faith will crumble when times get tough.

Our faith begins the moment we join God's family. That is our spiritual birth, the time when the Holy Spirit comes to live inside the believer as proof that he or she is a child of God. Then we begin living a new life by faith in Christ, exercising it like a muscle we want to build up. Over the years, as we follow Christ, our faith is strengthened and matured until it becomes vibrant and steady. That doesn't mean that sometimes God won't give us an extra measure of faith above our spiritual maturity level when we need it, but we are responsible for feeding and caring for our faith.

The Foundation of Faith

In the New Testament, the apostle Paul gives us the basis for our faith: "We Jewish Christians know that we become right with God, not by doing what the law commands, but by faith in Jesus Christ. So we have believed in Christ Jesus, that we might be accepted by God because of our faith in Christ" (Gal. 2:16).

I like to think of faith as a most precious jewel, a beautiful diamond, that God gives us when we accept His Son as our Savior. I'm sure you've heard the saying, "A diamond is a girl's best friend." This certainly is true in the case of our faith—a precious treasure. Faith is a believer's foundation. With it, we have access to all the riches in God's kingdom.

But you may be wondering why, if faith is so valuable, it doesn't seem very spectacular to you. There's a simple explanation. Diamonds are beautiful, yet when they are discovered in the original state, they look like pebbles. In fact, one of the largest diamond mining areas in the world—South Africa—began when a young boy picked up a shiny stone from the Orange River. He just stuck it in his pocket with the rest of his "treasures." But it turned out to be a 21-carat diamond![2]

Sometimes we don't understand the value of our faith. We are so conditioned by our culture to only deal with what we can see, touch, hear, feel and taste that we let God's supernatural life within us lie dormant. It settles deep like the pebble in the boy's pocket, unappreciated. But God is not content to let our faith in

Him remain hidden. Instead, He has a plan to help us increase our faith. He takes that rough stone and begins to bring out its true beauty. This is a process of cutting and shaping the stone until its beauty shines forth. Don't you want to have that kind of inner beauty?

God is very clear about the kind of faith He requires of us. Let me describe this faith for you with an example.

One of the advantages I have enjoyed over the years is getting to know the wonderful staff members God has led to join the mission organization Bill and I founded. Some of these men and women are the greatest thinkers in the Christian world. Dr. Joon Gon Kim was founder of Campus Crusade's Korean ministry, and he has served the Lord selflessly for many years. He has written an excellent article on faith that explains the complexity and the different aspects of our faith. He says that faith has three elements: intellectual, emotional and volitional. He writes:

> First, faith has an intellectual element. We must know who God is and that the Bible is God's Word. We also must know who Jesus is and what He has done for us. But knowing is not enough. Even the demons have great knowledge of God, yet they have no faith in God.
>
> Second, faith has an emotional element. The apostle Thomas confessed his faith in Jesus as "my Lord and my God." He was not in intellectual recognition of Jesus as Christ, but an emotional element was included. Emotions can vary and can at best be merely expressions of true faith. . . .
>
> Third, faith has a volitional element [or will], the personal application—accepting Jesus Christ as our Savior and Lord. John 1:12 says, "Yet to all who received him, to those who believed in his name, he gave the right to become children of God." This verse clearly indicates that the decision of receiving Him is up to each person's will.[3]

Faith is not complete without these three elements. But when complete, faith comprises the basis of our life with God. Dr. Kim goes on to say:

No area of the Christian life is divorced from faith. Faith is the source of all graces that we receive. We are saved by faith. We live by faith. We pray by faith. We walk by faith. We appropriate the filling of the Holy Spirit by faith. By faith we overcome the world. All these blessings and virtues of the Christian life are rooted in faith. The more we trust, obey, and faithfully serve God, the more we grow in our faith.[4]

Do you have all three elements of faith? Is your faith authentic and complete? Let me illustrate the importance of these three elements with an example.

One of the joys of parenthood is helping your children take on more adult-like responsibilities. But sometimes the journey to responsibility is not so smooth. That's what one single mother discovered when she found the police at her doorstep one day. Her 15-year-old daughter had wanted to drive so badly that she took the family van for a spin with her girlfriend. Yet the young girl had never had a driver's training class or passed a driver's test. She just took it upon herself—without permission—to take the vehicle. Half a block from home, she lost control of the van, ran through a picket fence, and into a tree. Thankfully, neither of the girls was injured, but the van was totaled. Because the daughter was an unlicensed driver and a family member, the auto insurance company was not obligated to pay for the damages. The family now not only has a payment for a replacement vehicle, but also for the unusable van!

Faith Needs a Mental Connection

What was the daughter's problem? She didn't have the knowledge and skill required to drive. In a similar way, no one can have faith without the right knowledge. Cults prove that. So many people believe in religious theories that are untrue. Because these people believe the wrong information or have a lack of information, they can't make informed decisions about their faith. The apostle Paul writes, "Faith comes from listening to this message of good news— the Good News about Christ" (Rom. 10:17).

Therefore, step one is hearing the message. Do you know the gospel message—that Jesus Christ came from heaven in the form of a man to die on a cross to pay for your sins? Have you heard the Good News that Jesus has provided the only way for us to become children of God?

When the young girl got behind the wheel of the van, she thought she knew how to drive. She was confident that she could accomplish what others told her was a dangerous activity for her. The consequences of her lack of knowledge were devastating to her and her family. The consequences of missing out on understanding God's message of Good News are even more dire. With faith in Christ, we are ushered into a life of joy and a destiny with Jesus. Without faith in Christ, we face eternal separation from God.

If you have never read or heard a clear explanation of how you can take a step of faith in Christ, turn to "Beginning Your Journey of Joy" at the end of this book and follow the information given. This will be the day you receive an authentic faith!

Faith Needs an Emotional Connection

But let's go on to the second element of faith—the emotional. This is an area that becomes a problem for many people. They know the plan of salvation as given in the Bible; they believe it is true, but they don't embrace the truth. The message never travels the few inches from their heads to their hearts.

When a teen begins to drive, he learns a lot of rules: Don't go over the speed limit. Don't follow too closely on the freeway. Check your rearview mirror frequently. Have you ever watched a teen nod his head, giving lip service to the rules, but you suspect that he's not taking them seriously? He's an accident waiting to happen.

Chris had been given all the usual lectures about safe driving, but his parents worried that he hadn't taken them to heart. They wondered what he would do when he was driving in a car with other teens. Would he race? Would he try to prove he was daring?

Then his drivers' education class watched a training video that showed the real-life results of teens who were speeding and had an accident—including all the bloody details. That day, Chris came home with a new attitude toward his driving. He had made an emotional connection with the rules of the road!

A person who has an authentic faith has also made an emotional connection—with her Savior and Lord, Jesus Christ. The facts have come alive! The message has touched her heart! That makes her faith a living, growing spirit within her, more than just inert facts on a page.

Now let's add the volitional element. This is where your will is involved. This means that you make a decision that involves more than a mere emotional response.

Chris had an emotional response to the training video, but that change of heart could easily fade with the passage of time. A year from now, will Chris still be motivated to drive safely by what he saw, or will he begin to take chances?

Faith Needs a Volitional Connection

Along with his emotional response, Chris must make safe driving a part of his core beliefs. He will then look for ways to become a better driver, which will naturally become a way of driving.

When you, as a matter of your will, accept Christ as your Savior and Lord, you begin a lifestyle of faith. The Holy Spirit comes into your life and is the Source of your faith. You are not building faith on your own. It becomes a supernatural adventure! The apostle Peter enthusiastically explains our relationship this way:

> Through Christ you have come to trust in God. And because God raised Christ from the dead and gave him great glory, your faith and hope can be placed confidently in God. . . . For you have been born again. Your new life did not come from your earthly parents because the life they gave you will end in death. But this new life will last forever because it comes from the eternal, living word of God (1 Pet. 1:21,23).

When I think about how much God loves me, and the sacrifice Jesus made on my behalf, I am overwhelmed. The facts are that

God loves me so much that my heart responds in the deepest way, causing me to place my whole trust in Him. That's faith—a combination of facts, emotions and will tied neatly together with "heartstrings."

If you have never made the decision to invite Christ into your life as Savior and Lord, read no further until you do! Turn to the "Beginning Your Journey of Joy" section at the back of the book and make sure you have true faith in Christ. If you have already taken this step, praise God for His graciousness and His unending love toward you.

A Pathway to Deepen My Faith

1. Learning from the Chapter
Which illustration from the chapter helped you understand the basics of faith best? Why?

_____

_____

_____

_____

_____

2. Knowing God's Word
Use the following verses to help you dig deeper into God's Word to learn more about faith. What similarities can you find between these two passages?

Mark 11:22-24

_____

_____

_____

_____

_____

_____

John 6:28-29

_____

_____

_____

_____

_____

3. Applying God's Word

All of us struggle with lapses in faith when our circumstances seem against us. What does the following verse tell us to do with our faith in tough times?

Ephesians 6:16

_____

_____

_____

_____

_____

What spiritual or physical battles have you faced in the past month? In the past year?

_____

_____

_____

_____

_____

_____

How could this verse help you manage the next crisis in your life? Be specific when you give this answer.

_____

_____

_____

_____

_____

_____

What does 1 Thessalonians 5:8 add to what Ephesians 6:16 tells us?

_____

_____

_____

_____

_____

_____

Can you think of a time when faith enabled you to think clearly? What happened?

_____

_____

_____

_____

_____

_____

Looking ahead to the future, how will being protected by faith and love help you to think clearly? Explain how you will act in faith the next time you have a financial or physical crisis. Make sure that prayer—talking with God—is part of your answer.

_____

_____

_____

_____

_____

_____

Notes
1. For a more detailed look at these concepts, see Lee Strobel, *The Case for Christ;* Josh McDowell, *Evidence that Demands a Verdict;* and the video *Unlocking the Secrets of Life* by Illustra Media.
2. Graham Rickard, *Spotlight on Diamonds* (Vero Beach, FL: Rourke Enterprises, 1988), pp. 20-21.
3. Joon Gon Kim, "Faith," in *Principles of Leadership* by Ted Martin and Michael Cozzins, comps. and eds. (Orlando, FL: NewLife Publications, 2001), pp. 17-18.
4. Ibid.

2

Moments of Faith

Our souls were made to "mount up with wings,"
and they can never be satisfied with anything short of flying.
Our souls chafe and fret, and cry out for freedom. [1]

HANNAH WHITALL SMITH

One difficulty we experience in living is the discouragement we sometimes feel when we can't see what God is doing in our life. Has that ever happened to you?

I remember one time, early in the ministry of Campus Crusade for Christ, when I felt like giving up. My involvement in the ministry had started out so positively. When Bill began working on the campus of UCLA, I was teaching school in Los Angeles. I decided that to share Bill's vision to reach others for Christ, I needed to quit my job and work full-time alongside him. He agreed enthusiastically. So that's what I did, and we saw tremendous fruit. He worked with the male coeds and I worked with the women. That first year, I saw 50 women come to faith in Jesus Christ. I helped train them to share their faith with others and to grow in their Christian walk. The experience was one of the most fulfilling I ever had.

Then Bill and I moved into the Bel Air mansion of Dr. Henrietta Mears, who was Christian Education Director at Hollywood Presbyterian Church. We were just minutes from the UCLA campus. This allowed us to expand our ministry to college students, and the traffic in the house mushroomed. How glorious to see all those young people meeting in our home—praying, singing, learning, and so enthusiastic about Jesus Christ!

But I didn't count on all the work that would become my responsibility. I had to clean the house, cook the food and clean up after the students left. Our Moorish "castle" was a huge place! And there were so many meetings. I went from being the one who trained the women to the one who was stuck in the kitchen. Bill kindly questioned how much time I had spent in Bible study that day. I reacted inwardly, *That's not my problem—I'm tired.*

Ultimately, Bill suggested that we hire a housekeeper to help with the work; so we did. Still, I was not finding the same fulfillment that I had experienced when working on campus. Trying to determine each day whether I would go to campus to minister or stay at home was a constant battle for me. In my frustration, I knew that I wasn't doing an adequate job in either place.

Then came the children. First Zac, our beautiful baby son. For a while, I found it fun to be at home, free from the meetings, playing a role as wife and mother. But after a few months, my opinion changed when I discovered that my "freedom" was really just a further round of responsibilities.

Then we were blessed with a second son, Brad. What a joyful event! But about the same time, our housekeeper left without notice. Because of the students who were living with us, and the many who were in and out of our home constantly, she found the housework too strenuous.

With each week that passed, I found myself more physically and emotionally drained. I was becoming a dissatisfied, critical, grumpy person. Repeatedly, I said to Bill, "Honey, we've got to move. I can't stand this house any longer. All day long I clean, cook and watch the children, and I can't take it anymore." Soon my husband, my children, Miss Mears, and the students were as irritating to me as the house itself.

A lovely house . . . a successful husband . . . an effective ministry . . . two beautiful sons. Wasn't this everything I'd dreamed and worked for? This wasn't fulfillment. Where was the confidence that my faith should give me? Why was I struggling so?

I knew that if I didn't find a solution, I was going to be a dissatisfied woman for a long time. Then one day God showed me that the problem was with my attitude. Almost every woman in ministry struggles with the same problems I had with the responsibilities of family and ministry. I read John 10:10, where Jesus says, "My purpose is to give life in all its fullness." This meant that He wanted me to have the most fulfilling life possible. He had a solution to my problem, but it wasn't going to be to give me the easy life.

Miss Mears suggested that I think of all my cares resting in the palm of my left hand, weighing me down and robbing me of all my joy, even to the security of my relationship with God. She then suggested that I think of God as my right hand and physically transfer all of the cares in my left hand into my right hand as a gift to God. Just turn loose and let Him carry the burdens.

He wanted me to cast all my cares on Him, to let Him satisfy my needs and care for me. "Give all your worries and cares to God, for he cares about what happens to you" (1 Pet. 5:7). This was a new attitude for me! Instead of solving my problems myself by "working smarter and harder," I could trust God with everything and let Him work it all out. God began to give me solutions, such as allowing some of the students to help me prepare food or clean up after a meal. Most were more than willing to help. Little by little, God turned my situation around as I turned my problems over to Him.

Amazingly, He then led me to begin sharing with women's groups, particularly pastors' wives, about my own search concerning my lack of fulfillment. I openly admitted the problems and defeats that I had experienced, and most important, the solutions He had given me. How satisfying to hear other women say, "Thank you for admitting your weaknesses and sharing the answers God gave you. I am struggling with the same problems." From this response, I began to realize that sharing these solutions made my difficult experiences seem even more worthwhile. I was able to encourage other women!

What happened to me during that time is what I like to call "a moment of faith." This is a time—it could be an instantaneous realization or a more gradual recognition—when a person sees what God is doing in her life. What I saw at that moment was that God was stretching my faith and asking me to place my situation in

His hands. He was using me and molding me, but I needed to be willing and pliable. My responsibility was to give up some of my "rights" to allow God to work for my greater good and the good of others. It wasn't that God was doing more or less at that moment in time, but that I finally saw His purposes.

I have divided moments of faith into three categories:

1. Stretching my faith
2. Encouraging my faith
3. Recognizing my lack of faith

These are not biblical principles, but just a way for me to explain more clearly what God is doing in my life.

It is wonderful to reflect on the "faith moments" in my life, but even more exciting to think about all the people who have served as staff members of Campus Crusade and recall some of the faith moments that changed the course of their entire future.

Catherine's Moment of Faith

This young woman's words capture for me the commitment that typifies a Campus Crusade staff member:

> It was my last year of college. I had the wonderful opportunity to attend a Christmas Conference sponsored by Campus Crusade for Christ at Arrowhead Springs in the mountains of Southern California. The main speaker for this conference was Elmer Lappen, a man suffering from crippling arthritis and confined to a wheelchair. Sitting in a room with about a thousand students, I listened as he gave a final challenge on the last day of his series on discipleship. Quoting Isaiah 6:8, Elmer issued the call. He then said that if we wanted to be sold out to Jesus Christ, to go where He led, and do what He asked, that we were to stand, state our name and say, "Here am I, Lord, send me." It was a moment etched in time for me. I watched as young

people all around the room began to stand, state their name, and respond to God. My heart was beating fast. Now was the moment for me. I stood and said, "My name is Catherine. Here am I, Lord. Send me!"

Catherine Martin is now a Director of Women's Ministries and founder and President of Quiet Time Ministries, a worldwide ministry teaching devotion to God and His Word. Catherine's moment of faith changed her life.

Have you experienced these moments of faith in your life? What happened? Was it uplifting, scary, humbling, awesome? Let's look at some moments of faith in the lives of several other believers.

Stretching Your Faith

Faith moments become an integral part of our lives when we let the Spirit control us. Let me give you an example of what I mean about each category—stretching faith, encouraging faith and recognizing lack of faith—beginning with stretching your faith. Stretching your faith is a time when you can feel discouraged or overwhelmed, or you can feel enthusiastic. It all depends on your attitude.

When a cook makes pizza dough, she begins with a round ball of flour, water and yeast. It doesn't look like much. But then she begins to roll out the dough and stretch it with her hands. An expert pizza maker can stretch the dough to cover a large pizza pan without tearing the dough. Her fingers and fists deftly work around the circle to enlarge it gradually. Then she lets the dough rest a few moments on the pan before finishing the pie.

God knows just how He wants your character to stretch and grow for you to become more godly. He puts you in situations that stretch your character and help you build those qualities in your life that please Him.

What stretching moments have you experienced? Many of those stretching moments probably weren't too pleasant at the time, but their result was gratifying.

Amy Carmichael had one of those faith moments. She grew up in Northern Ireland in the last half of the nineteenth century. She had a wonderful childhood as a member of a large and loving family. Her parents had a deep faith in Jesus Christ, and they passed their faith on to their children.

When Amy was three years old, she had one wish above all others. Her mother had beautiful blue eyes, but Amy had brown ones. With all her heart, Amy wanted blue eyes.

Her mother had told her many times, "Ask God, Amy, if you want anything badly. Share it with Him. He's never too far away to hear our prayers, and He'll always give you an answer."[2]

Amy believed that God would answer her prayers, so she asked Him to change her eye color to blue. Then she went to bed. She was absolutely sure that the next morning she would wake up with blue eyes.

As soon as she woke up the next morning, she pushed a chair over to the chest of drawers and climbed up on the seat so that she could see herself in the bureau mirror. Reflected back at her was a brown-eyed little face. God had not changed her eye color.

At first she was disappointed, but then she realized that no was an answer to prayer just as much as yes was. She was content to let her wise God have His way.

Many years later, Amy traveled to India as a missionary. While she was there, she saw the poor, abused children who had been sold as slaves to the temple. Amy determined to rescue these children and bring them up in a Christian atmosphere.

She devised a plan. She stained her arms, hands and face with coffee to make herself look like an Indian woman, and she covered herself with an Indian sari so that she could pass into the temple where foreigners were not allowed to go. She would then take the children away with her and liberate them from their slavery.

One day, she recognized a gracious truth about her success in rescuing so many children. If her eyes had been blue instead of brown, she could not have escaped detection in the temple. God had known from the day He formed her that she needed brown eyes! Many times, she told this story to her Indian children, encouraging them to have faith in God too.

As a little girl, Amy's faith was stretched through her prayer. Yet she didn't understand all the ramifications of what God was doing until many years later. Her faith was stretched to accept the answer to her prayer. Her faith was rewarded in seeing Him use her in so many children's lives.

Sometimes we may resent faith-stretching experiences. But they are really blessings. We may never know in this life what God was doing during these times, but we can be sure that His hands are gently forming us into women usable for His kingdom!

Encouraging Your Faith

Have you ever felt that you have made a sacrifice for God without seeing the immediate outcome? For most of us, we obey God, not because of what we think might happen, but because we know that's what God wants us to do. That's the attitude of young Peter ten Boom. He was the nephew of Corrie ten Boom, the woman who achieved fame for helping to hide Jewish people during World War II. The ten Boom house, a short ride from Amsterdam in the Netherlands, became a safe house to which Jewish refugees could escape from the Nazis.

When Dutch patriots learned that the dreaded SS troops were systematically raiding orphanages and taking Jewish children, then sending them to their death in the concentration camps of Europe, brave Dutch men impersonated SS officers at the risk of their lives, raided the orphanages and took the Jewish babies to the ten Boom house. Then the babies were sent to safe houses and farms where non-Jewish Dutch citizens adopted them as their own. Only God knows how many children were saved, but their numbers were in the hundreds before the Germans finally raided the ten Boom home and sent members of the family to prison. At about the same time, Peter was also arrested and sent to prison. He was only 16 years old.

Although many of his family members died, Peter survived the ordeal under the Nazis, and after the war, he went throughout the world with the same message as his famous Aunt Corrie: Forgiveness is the only answer to hatred that never dies.

Many years later, while Peter was on a speaking tour in Israel, he had a heart attack. Going home was out of the question. Immediate surgery was needed to save his life. As the cardiologist chatted with Peter before the operation, he said, "I see your name is ten Boom. Hmm. Are you by any chance related to the ten Booms of Holland?"

"Yes," Peter replied. "That is my family."

The doctor got excited. "And I am one of the babies that your family saved!"[3]

At that moment, God pulled back the curtain on His mysterious ways and showed Peter ten Boom just a sliver of what Peter had accomplished by obeying God, even when it nearly cost him his life! Now Peter's life was being saved by the very person he had had a part in saving years ago. What an encouraging moment of faith!

You, too, will find moments of faith to encourage your walk with God. Perhaps the encouragement will come from the way God works out circumstances, how He answers prayer or how He protects you in the midst of trouble. These really are special moments in our Christian life. We can remember them and treasure them forever.

Recognizing Your Lack of Faith

Hadassah lost her parents when she was young, so she had been raised by a kindly uncle. She was part of a minority community; therefore, sometimes she didn't feel well-accepted in her city. She had a lot of strikes against her, but she put her mind to achieving success in spite of her situation. She decided to do what it took to attain her goals. Because of her natural abilities and her faith in God, she reached the top of the ladder in her field.

Do you know any women like this? Their beauty and confidence come from their walk with God developed over the years. Hadassah's life was a testimony to what God can do with a woman willing to be used by Him.

Do you recognize Hadassah's story? The Bible also calls her Esther, and there's a book named after her in the Old Testament. She's the woman who became the queen of Persia during the reign of King Xerxes, a ruler who commanded an empire that spanned from India to Ethiopia. Esther was chosen to be queen because of her beauty, but she kept one fact hidden from the king—that she belonged to the Jewish race, a people who had been conquered and taken captive by the Persians. Some of the Israelites had been exiled from Jerusalem to Babylon. Esther's family had suffered this fate. That's why she kept her heritage a secret.

Doesn't this sound like a set-up for a cloak-and-dagger plot in a novel? But this happened in real life. God had taken an unknown Jewish girl and placed her in the most coveted spot in the kingdom.

Soon, a man named Haman hatched a plot against all the Jews. He was a virile anti-Semite and wanted to be rid of them all. He beguiled the king into signing a decree that all the Jews—even the women and children—would be slaughtered on a single day. The date was set on the royal calendar. It was coming up fast.

Esther's uncle sent her a message of desperation. "You're the Queen! You're the only one who can save our people. Go to the king and beg for the lives of our people."

"But, Mordecai," she lamented, "the king has not asked me to come into his presence for many days. If I go uninvited, I could lose my life!"

What a dilemma this situation posed for Esther. Everyone admired her. She lived in luxury. Who had things better than she did? This would all change for the worse if she revealed her Jewish identity.

This problem brought about a moment of faith for Esther. The decision she had to make was this: Would she trust her life into God's hands and bravely go to the king to plead for her people? Or would she keep silent and hope that she would be protected on that horrible day?

Mordecai advised Esther: "If you keep quiet at a time like this, deliverance for the Jews will arise from some other place, but you and your relatives will die. What's more, who can say but that you have been elevated to the palace for just such a time as this?" (Esther 4:14).

Mordecai's faith in God was strong. He believed God's promise that God wouldn't desert His people—ever. But Esther's faith wasn't as strong.

She asked Mordecai to tell all the Israelites to fast and pray for what she was about to do. She was willing to die trying to save her people, but her knees were shaking.

The people prayed for three days, then Esther went to the king to make her request. She invited him and Haman to a banquet where she planned to reveal Haman's trickery and evil.

But at the banquet, Esther chickened out at the last minute. She didn't have the strength to speak out; her faith was too weak. But she did invite the men to a second banquet the next night.

Think of what agony this delay must have been for Mordecai and the Jewish people who were praying!

The same problem arose at the second banquet. Esther chickened out and invited the two men to a third night. They accepted. In fact, Haman was honored. The queen was giving him special attention!

Have you ever found yourself in a situation where your faith was inadequate? God puts us through these tests so that we can recognize where we are weak in our faith and where He wants us to exercise our faith muscle. We have the choice; He provides the strength when we say, "Yes, Lord!"

That's what Esther finally did. She spoke up, admitting that she was Jewish and explained how evil Haman's plans were. The result? Haman was executed and the Jews were saved! Today, the Jewish people celebrate the Feast of Purim to honor Esther's courage and faith.

Just like Esther, God puts you in a place that He has prepared beforehand. You are the only one who can do what He has laid out for you to do. When you step forth in faith—success. If you step back in fear or doubt—failure. Remember, success is to do what pleases God, not to go along with the value system of the world.

You can probably think back to times when you missed the faith mark, and other times when God gave you success through your faith. How did you feel after each time? What were the long-term ramifications of each? If you examine how you dealt with each moment of recognizing your faith, you will see that your decision—either way—sent ripples of consequences into your future.

So now that you are beginning to understand how valuable your faith is, we can begin to look at the beauty of the diamond of faith we hold in our hands. Just as a diamond has facets, so does faith. Let's look at several of these facets:

- A knowing faith
- A living faith
- A loving faith
- A serving faith
- A giving faith
- A sharing faith
- A rewarding faith

Each of these presents a different element to our faith. Just as a diamond that is cut in half would not have the same fire or brilliance, our faith needs all these elements to be complete. As we grow in our faith, we can work to have a balance in our Christian walk. We will also have the fire of God's holiness at work in our life. I love how Charles Swindoll expresses the results of living by faith: "Your faith ought to get you in trouble at times."[4]

My husband, Bill, felt hope and freedom in the midst of his suffering. I experienced it by his side. Did my faith withstand? Oh, yes! It went beyond endurance. It was freedom and joy and security. To this day, I can confidently say that God not only brought my husband through until he made his journey to heaven, but He did the same for me.

This can all be yours as well. Take a walk of faith with me to discover all that God has laid out for you—the fullness of life, the eternal rewards, the blessings here and now, the wisdom of the ages. It's the only way to live.

A Pathway to Deepen Your Faith

Learning from the Chapter
Have you ever experienced a time when God stretched your faith?
What happened?

_____

_____

_____

_____

_____

_____

_____

Have you ever experienced a time when a fellow believer encouraged you in your faith? How did you feel?

_____

_____

_____

_____

_____

_____

When we lack faith, our circumstances go from hard to even more
difficult. Describe a time when this happened to you. How did the
crisis turn out?

_____

_____

_____

_____

_____

_____

Knowing God's Word
Read each verse, then meditate on how it can help you build your
faith in the areas mentioned.

Stretching your faith: Hebrews 11:6

_____
_____
_____
_____
_____
_____

Encouraging your faith: James 1:5

_____
_____
_____
_____
_____
_____

Recognizing your lack of faith: James 1:6

_____
_____
_____
_____
_____
_____

Applying God's Word
Do you have a faith crisis confronting you right now? Into which
of the three categories would you place it?

_____
_____
_____
_____
_____

What steps will you take to help you keep your faith secure through this crisis?

_____

_____

_____

_____

_____

_____

_____

Read Romans 5:1. Use this verse to help you understand how faith will help you during any crisis, and record your answer.

_____

_____

_____

_____

_____

_____

_____

Notes
1. Hannah Whitall Smith, *The Christian's Secret of a Happy Life* (Uhrichsville, OH: Barbour Publishing 2001), p. 33.
2. Kathleen White, *Amy Carmichael* (Minneapolis, MN: Bethany House Publishers, 1986), pp. 7-9.
3. Harold Sala, *Profiles of Faith* (Grand Rapids, MI: Kregel Publications, n.d.).
4. Charles R. Swindoll, *The Tale of the Oxcart* (Nashville, TN: Word Publishing, 1988), p. 195.

3

A Knowing Faith

*There are three things indispensable to faith—knowledge, assent,
and appropriation. We must know God. "And this is eternal life, that they
might know Thee the only true God, and Jesus Christ, whom Thou hast
sent" (John 17:3). Then we must not only give our assent to what we know,
but we must lay hold of the truth. If a man simply gives his assent to the plan
of salvation, it will not save him; he must accept Christ as his Savior.
We must receive and appropriate him.*

D. L. MOODY

Veronica frantically ran around toward the back of the house while
chasing the family's miniature Doberman pinscher. She gripped a
letter in her hand. She had made up her mind to do it today. She
was leaving her husband. She couldn't stand the atmosphere in
her home anymore, or her own feelings of guilt and the constant
arguing. She had to get out! She was in such a state of emotion
that not once had she considered the impact her actions would
have on her two elementary-age children.

As she disappeared around the back of the house, a car sped
up the driveway. It was Veronica's husband, Frank, who had come
home from work after getting a call from his wife that she was leaving. Toni, a coworker, was with him. Toni had never met Veronica,
but she had been concerned about Frank's state of mind during
the past few days. Several of the other Christian employees at the
mortgage company where Toni and Frank worked were trying to
help him through this difficult time and were talking to him about
the Lord. When Frank asked Toni to come talk with his wife, she
had instantly agreed. But she had never been thrust into a family

crisis like this before. She really didn't know what to do or say. As the car came to a stop in the driveway, Toni sent a few more desperate prayers heavenward.

As Frank jumped out of the car and began searching for his wife, Toni stood in the driveway, unsure of what to do. Finally, she went inside the house. There was Veronica, standing in the living room, still clutching the good-bye letter.

Veronica stared at Toni, thinking, *Who is this stranger in my house? How does she dare to come in here? Why would Frank bring her here? To talk to me? She knows nothing about what I've been through . . . homeless as a child . . . an alcoholic parent . . .* But seeing her chance to get this women to deliver her bad news to Frank, she waved the letter at Toni, saying, "I don't know who you are, but I'm giving this 'Dear John' letter to you to give to my husband."

Toni stared at the white envelope. She didn't know what to say. But the words just came out: "Wait until Frank comes in. You need to talk to him yourself."

At that moment, Frank entered the living room, out of breath. When he saw the two women facing each other, he stopped abruptly. After an awkward pause, the three of them sat down to talk over the situation.

"Don't give him the letter now," Toni said calmly as she gently took the letter from Veronica. "Pray with me first." She was shaking as she led the way for the three of them to hold hands. As she prayed, calmness spread throughout the room.

When she raised her head after the prayer, Veronica said, "Okay, I'll stay for now."

Toni got up and left the two of them to continue talking out their problems.

The tense atmosphere in the house only increased after that time of prayer. Veronica, who was struggling with alcohol and drug abuse, was still determined to leave her family. She and Frank argued throughout that afternoon, their voices getting louder and louder as their children looked on with fearful eyes.

The next day, right in the middle of a heated argument, the couple heard a knock on the door. When Veronica opened the door, she saw three people from Toni's church standing outside. Desperate for help, she invited them in.

After introducing themselves, the three visitors began to talk to Frank and Veronica about Jesus Christ and how they could find peace and joy in a new life in Him. This was the first time Veronica had heard the gospel message explained in such a clear way. She had never understood how much God loved her and wanted her to be a part of His family. This was music to her aching heart.

Before the three visitors concluded their visit, Veronica was ready to place her faith in Jesus. She prayed with all her heart, asking God to forgive her sins and help her start her life anew. She didn't want to drink or use drugs anymore, and she wanted Him to take the weight of these things off her back.

What a change came over Veronica's household when her attitude made a 180-degree turn! Peace descended on the household, and Veronica's old feelings about leaving the family evaporated. Two days later, Frank also received Christ as his Savior, and the family began attending church. Within a few weeks, the children's Sunday School teachers had led both of them to faith in Christ.

If you talked to Veronica today, you would see the joy of Christ in her deep brown eyes and her sparkling smile. She exudes a liveliness she never had before, because she feels secure in God's love. As a child, she had experienced so much hardship that she was left with only feelings of worthlessness. But now she has that fullness of life that only God can give! She is optimistic about the future—no matter what she and her family have to face—because she has Jesus by her side. She and Frank have been working on their marital difficulties, and they have made tremendous progress. They have seen miraculous answers to prayer and are growing in their faith.

This is how a knowing faith transforms lives. As women, we touch the hearts of so many others, but we can only touch them with love and joy when Jesus spreads His love through us. Knowing Jesus is the secret to living life to the fullest. Just as Veronica would tell you, knowing Jesus makes life worth living! If you have never taken this most important step, read "Beginning Your Journey of

Joy" at the end of this book. Accepting Christ as your Savior will be the greatest step you will ever take in this life!

The "Knowing" Process

In the first section of this book, we learned that knowing and receiving the gospel message is the first step to faith, which results in a new life in Christ. But this knowing process goes on throughout our Christian life. Once we become children of God, we then spend our lifetime getting to know the Father God and His Son, Jesus Christ, who love us so much. Knowing God and having a close relationship with Him is the greatest pleasure anyone can ever experience.

Before I became a believer, I had ideas about God and faith, but most of them were off base. In the three years that I was engaged to Bill, I had time to analyze his life, my life and the lives of his new friends. I came to some interesting conclusions. For one, I was convinced that the faith Bill and his friends proclaimed was just a temporary phase and would soon pass. In fact, I was staking my future on this hope. Bill demonstrated a total commitment to his faith in Jesus Christ, and his sincerity was alarming to me. Along with the gifts Bill sent me, he also included passages of Scripture for me to read and specific prayer items for me to pray. At the time, I was questioning the depth of my faith and certainly didn't have confidence in my prayers. When Bill told me about answers to prayer that he had received, I felt even more insecure about my prayer life. Not only did I begin to question my prayer life, but I also doubted the validity of my faith.

I was so concerned about the future that I traveled to California for the purpose of helping Bill realize the error of his ways. Bill had given me a beautiful engagement ring at Christmas, and we announced plans for a September wedding. Before I left my dorm, I made a strong commitment to my college best friend that if I couldn't convince Bill that he was headed down a wrong path, I would come home without my engagement ring. That's how serious I thought the situation was.

That set up the greatest turning point of my life. How grateful I am to God that He saw me wandering in my confusion and brought me to Dr. Mears, a dear friend of Bill's. She gently explained to me how to know God personally. That day, I went from existing in darkness to living in light. Why? Because I learned who God really is—a God of love and mercy—and what He had done for me—sent His Son, Jesus, to die on a cross to pay the penalty of my sin. I read and reread Romans 10:9-13:

> For if you confess with your mouth that Jesus is Lord and believe in your heart that God raised him from the dead, you will be saved. For it is by believing in your heart that you are made right with God, and it is by confessing with your mouth that you are saved. As the Scriptures tell us, "Anyone who believes in him will not be disappointed." Jew and Gentile are the same in this respect. They all have the same Lord, who generously gives His riches to all who ask for them. For "Anyone who calls on the name of the Lord will be saved."

The word "saved" is a traditional expression that means an individual has been made right with God and has the assurance of heaven and eternal life.

Following my discussion with Miss Mears, I realized that the teachings about God that I had learned as a child were not all correct. Those that were wrong (that good works will get a person to heaven, for example) lost their relevance and meaning. A mysterious process was at work in my heart. The Holy Spirit was opening my eyes to God's truth, and I was learning about God.

What a change there was in my life! I had joy and peace, and I saw real answers to prayer. Bill and I set our wedding date, and I returned home with the diamond ring on my finger and a song in my heart expressing the joy of my faith.

On December 30, 1948, Bill and I were married in Oklahoma.

I must confess that life has never been the same since I received Christ as my Savior. I became a new person!

But I still had old attitudes to change and a lot of learning to do. One advantage I had now, though, was that I had the Holy Spirit in my life to lead, guide and teach me. And He was about to show me some of the areas in my life that weren't pleasing to God.

A knowing faith means that we are open to the Holy Spirit's teaching all the time. It means seeking God's will and principles (His ways) above all else. We cannot do this without focused effort. Having a knowing faith means searching for God's truth. That should become a part of our lifestyle of Christian living.

If you know God personally, He will help you in this process by showing you where you need to develop your faith. He has been so gracious in the way He has dealt with my areas of stubbornness. I especially remember one moment of faith when God encouraged me to place my trust in Him for my future in ways I never thought I could.

It happened when my teaching career was developing and Bill was in the final weeks of seminary. At that time, God gave him the vision for Campus Crusade for Christ, an organization designed to take the claims of Christ to college students and ultimately to the entire world. He was excited that God had revealed what He wanted him to do.

When I heard about Bill's vision, I was apprehensive, although I was careful not to let Bill know my fears or to deflate his dream. In my mind's eye, I could see everything we had talked about, dreamed of and hoped for fading into oblivion. Bill had started a fancy foods business that was growing immensely and raking in profits. Within a few years, we were going to be able to afford everything I wanted. Both of us had expensive appetites, and material possessions meant a great deal to us. Now Bill was talking about selling our business, moving to the UCLA campus and living by faith. Imagine that! I didn't know anyone who lived by faith in the extravagant fashion I wanted to live.

I began to think of other alternatives to Bill's plan. Secretly, I hoped we couldn't sell the business, and I figured we could test whether or not the vision for Campus Crusade for Christ was from God by asking an exorbitant price for the business.

After discussing it with Bill, he let me set the price. Much to my surprise, the first caller, a man familiar with the business, bought it. We could come up with no human explanation for its sale, either for the amount for which it was sold or for the speed with which it was sold. Surely, this was a confirmation from the Lord that He was leading us to start the ministry with students. You can imagine how this experience in faith gave me confidence in what God was doing in our lives!

I love the way Paul explains the process of knowing in Ephesians 2:8-9:

> God saved you by his special favor when you believed. And you can't take credit for this; it is a gift from God. Salvation is not a reward for the good things we have done, so none of us can boast about it. For we are God's masterpiece. He has created us anew in Christ Jesus, so that we can do the good things he planned for us long ago.

I was learning how God works in our lives. Before I was a Christian, I believed I had to earn God's favor. Now I knew that He first loved me and that He had something planned for my life beyond what I could even dream. My faith was beginning to stretch into a shape that God could use.

But perhaps you are wondering how anyone can know God. God has shown us the way.

Knowing God

Have you ever taken a personality test? The marketplace is filled with all types. Some tests are used by employers to fit workers into the right job positions. Others are used for couples in premarital counseling. Some are just for fun—to get to know yourself. Women's magazines often carry these personality tests in various forms.

Here in the ministry of Campus Crusade, we use certain tests to help staff members find the place where they can minister to others in the most effective and satisfying way. We realize, of course, that nothing replaces the leading of the Holy Spirit, but people are helped by knowing their areas of strengths and weaknesses and their spiritual gifts.

You may be wondering, *How do I get to know God? We can't give Him a personality test! He's so far out there, above us, unknowable, and mysterious.* It is true that if God didn't choose to reveal Himself to us, we would never be able to know Him. Our limitations are too great. But He does want us to get to know Him, so He has revealed a wealth of information about Himself. God has chosen to show Himself to us through two avenues: creation and the Bible. They are our primary sources of information. Through creation, God reveals His awesome splendor and majesty. Modern science just keeps uncovering more and more of God's creativity and beauty. In the Bible, God reveals to us the way He relates to us—through the message and life of His Son, Jesus, and through our communication with Him in prayer. These four avenues form the basis of our knowledge about God and how He works in our lives. Let's look at how each of these reveals God's character to us.

Creation

Have you ever noticed how scholars will study a painting or a novel to find out more about the painter or author? The personality of the creator comes through the creation.

Psalm 19:1-4 says, "The heavens tell of the glory of God. The skies display his marvelous craftsmanship. Day after day they continue to speak; night after night they make him known. They speak without a sound or a word; their voice is silent in the skies; yet their message has gone out to all the earth, and their words to all the world."

What do I see when I gaze at God's creation? His power and beauty. His orderliness and diversity. His wonder and awe. God says that they are a witness to us that He is alive and is in control of the universe. Creation is one of the best evidences that God exists.

The Bible

The other way we can discover God is through studying His nature—His revelation of Himself—as recorded in His Word. We call God's characteristics His holy attributes. Let me list just a few and Scriptures that tell about each:

- God is love—1 John 4:8
- God is merciful—Psalm 37:26
- God is eternal—Deuteronomy 33:27
- God does not change—Malachi 3:6
- God is holy—Isaiah 6:3
- God is faithful—1 Corinthians 1:9

I could give so many more. The study of God and His attributes is a lifelong journey. Even then, we will only scratch the surface of our unfathomably complex heavenly Father. If you would like to read more about God's attributes, Bill wrote an excellent book on the topic called *God: Discover His Character,* and the content is also available online at www.DiscoverGod.com.

Another aspect of knowing God through His Word is getting to know the truths and principles that God considers essential. That, of course, involves studying your Bible. Within its pages is the manual for living a holy life. If you have never studied the Bible on your own, you can find many excellent Bible study tools at your local Christian bookstore.

Jesus, His Son

If you have children, you can be sure that people are getting to know something about you from your children. They can see your biological traits in them. Your children carry along your traditions and heritage. Sadly, our kids also pick up our bad habits. But they can also make us proud by how they serve the Lord.

In a similar way, we get to know God through knowing His Son. Therefore, along with getting to know God, a knowing faith also means getting to know Jesus. As God's Son, He is the form of God revealed in the flesh. Jesus Himself said to one of His disciples:

Philip, don't you even yet know who I am, even after all the time I have been with you? Anyone who has seen me has seen the Father! So why are you asking to see him? Don't you believe that I am in the Father and the Father is in me? The words I say are not my own, but my Father who lives in me does his work through me. Just believe that I am in the Father and the Father is in me. Or at least believe because of what you have seen me do (John 14:9-11).

Whatever Jesus did, He was expressing the character of the Father, doing so in the Father's will and in the power of the Holy Spirit. The acts of kindness Jesus did, the healing miracles He performed, His wise teaching were all part of the Father's plan.

Prayer

Because knowing also involves emotions, we get to know God by responding to Him as His child. That's why prayer—communication with God—is essential to a knowing faith.

Do you remember your dating days? (Maybe you're still there!) Communication loomed mighty large. You were desperate to get to know that person. Extended telephone calls, long letters, evenings spent talking about the minutia of life, even just looking into each other's eyes without saying a word. How much more should we want to spend time in God's presence! One of the ways we do that is by worshiping Him in our local church service or through Bible reading and praises. Our prayer life is another way we respond to Him.

Arthur T. Pierson describes how important it is to have a continuing faith based on our knowledge of God: "As long as we are able to trust God, holding fast in heart, that he is able and willing to help those who rest on the Lord Jesus for salvation, in all matters which are for His glory and their good, the heart remains calm and peaceful. It is only when we practically let go of our faith in His power or His love that we lose our peace and become troubled."[1]

We can sum up the process of knowing God in faith by practicing these steps:

- Meet God daily in a devotional time.
- Communicate frequently with God through prayer.
- Study God's Word on a consistent basis.
- Worship God with others at your church, and when you are alone.

Beverly LaHaye, founder of Concerned Women of America, puts this into perspective when she says, "Know what the Bible says, know why you believe what you do believe. You've got convictions; then find out why you have those convictions. Support them with Scripture. If they are God-instilled convictions, you cannot remain passive and not do anything about them. And then, allow the Holy Spirit to work in your life."[2]

With a foundation in a knowing faith, we can then go on to build a living faith!

A Pathway to Deepen My Faith

1. Learning from the Chapter

Describe in a couple of sentences what you know about God.

_____
_____
_____
_____
_____
_____

What about God is easy for you to understand, and what is difficult?

_____
_____
_____
_____
_____

2. Knowing God's Word

Read Philippians 3:9. How does this verse describe how I can get right with God?

_____

_____

_____

_____

_____

_____

Read the story of the Roman officer in Matthew 8:5-13. What knowledge did the officer have about Jesus?

_____

_____

_____

_____

_____

How did that knowledge help him?

_____

_____

_____

_____

_____

3. Applying God's Word

What amazes you about the story you just read in Matthew 8?

_____

_____

_____

_____

_____

How can you use that incident in the life of Jesus to encourage your faith?

_____

_____

_____

_____

_____

_____

_____

To get to know God better, look up these titles in a Bible concordance: Almighty God, Eternal God, Jehovah, Lord of Hosts, Father, Holy One. What does each name say about the character of God the Father?

_____

_____

_____

_____

_____

_____

_____

Notes

1. Arthur T. Pierson, *George Muller of Bristol and His Witness to a Prayer-Hearing God* (New York: Loizeaux Brothers, 1899), p. 437.
2. As quoted by Helen Kooiman Hosier, *100 Christian Women Who Changed the 20ᵗʰ Century* (Grand Rapids, MI: Fleming H. Revell, 2000), p. 223.

4

A Living Faith

It is your living faith in the adequacy of the One who is in you,
which releases His divine action through you.

W. IAN THOMAS

If you've ever taken a trip to Europe as a sightseer, you probably visited some of the gorgeous churches and cathedrals in that area of the world. The buildings are worth seeing. With their ornate domes and spires, their intricate façades and imposing towers, they rise above the cityscapes. Inside, the cathedrals are dressed in marble and are clothed in stained glass that showers the onlooker with a rainbow of light. In the Chartres Cathedral in France, for example, the resplendent rose window and the stained glass panel, Our Lady of the Beautiful Window, are stunning. Deep reds and blues frame the face of Jesus the King in the Our Lady window, while the design of the rose window glass shines like living jewels. But sadly today in the great churches of Europe the congregations are dwindling and many of the most magnificent buildings are merely museums. When you walk under their arched roofs, all you hear are echoes. The living faith they once embraced has died.

Contrast their stilled beauty with the "army of worms" of China. These are believers who have little of this world's goods, but they are rich in faith. They meet in houses to avoid persecution from their government, but still they are not afraid to suffer for their faith. Some have been imprisoned for decades! They believe the hardships they have endured are their training ground—to be an army of worms! Their plan is to make their way from their homes in China to Jerusalem as evangelists, taking the gospel to the peoples living between China and Jerusalem. This includes some of the most difficult places in which to witness for your faith, including India, Saudia Arabia and Iran.

In the book *Back to Jerusalem*, the house church leaders describe their plan:

> This is how the Chinese Christians will operate during the Back to Jerusalem mission. We will not make much noise, but will secretly and quietly do the Lord's work underground. We will be quite difficult to detect. You may not hear many victorious reports of church growth coming back from the Middle East or Southeast Asia, but be assured that our ants, worms, and termites are already there, quietly working away, slowly loosening the foundations of Islam, Buddhism, and Hinduism. You will not see any great or small church buildings resulting from our efforts because we are determined to do what the Lord has led us to do in China these past fifty years and establish spiritual fellowships of believers who meet in their homes. We won't build a single church building anywhere, but the Lord will be building up his church of living stones, with Jesus as the cornerstone.[1]

The cathedrals represent a faith that is no longer alive, but has slipped into tradition and history. They're like corpses, only a shell of their former life. Although they are beautiful, they have none of the Holy Spirit within them. But the Chinese believers are full of spiritual life. Their faith is growing and spreading. It is alive!

Just a word of caution: I am not suggesting that there is a correlation between the size of a church's building and the size of its spiritual impact. I know of many churches with wonderful facilities that are thriving and obeying God in faith. But to these churches, the buildings are vehicles to advance God's kingdom, not monuments to man's artistic successes. A living faith does not depend on any exterior props for its vibrancy. Not on how we dress, the background of our family, how much money we have in the bank, which side of town we come from or where we worship.

Not whether we get our hair styled in a salon or do it ourselves. Or wear off-the-rack dresses or designer clothing. God is looking for an army of faithful women who will put Him above the routine of life, over the material possession they may desire, even above their families and friends. God is looking for those few who will live totally for Him.

Our living faith relies on the Holy Spirit's work in the life of each individual Christian. This is the heritage of every woman in Christ!

The Vine and the Branches

Jesus gives us a picture of how a living faith works. This is what He says about Himself:

> I am the true vine, and my Father is the gardener. He cuts off every branch that doesn't produce fruit, and he prunes the branches that do bear fruit so they will produce even more. You have already been pruned for greater fruitfulness by the message I have given you. Remain in me, and I will remain in you. For a branch cannot produce fruit if it is severed from the vine, and you cannot be fruitful apart from me. Yes, I am the vine; you are the branches. Those who remain in me, and I in them, will produce much fruit. For apart from me you can do nothing (John 15:1-5).

Ask the Vermont maple grower what the most important part of the tree is and he'll tell you it's the sap. When he puts in the plug in the spring, the delicious amber syrup drips into the pail. From the maple sap, he produces his maple syrup and candy.

Every part of every plant is dependent on the process of the sap coming up and bringing water and nutrients to the branches. Every trembling leaf of every maple tree is connected to this life-giving process. If the farmer cuts off a tree branch, it quickly withers and dies. Why? Because it is no longer connected to its life source.

Jesus is our spiritual life source. He has sent His Spirit to take up permanent residence in our bodies and souls. It is through Him that we produce the living fruit of God. Galatians 5:22-23 tells us:

> But when the Holy Spirit controls our lives, he will produce this kind of fruit in us: love, joy, peace, patience, kindness, goodness, faithfulness, gentleness, and self-control.

The Bible says that the process of letting the Spirit of Christ produce fruit in our lives is called being filled with the Spirit. The apostle Paul writes, "Don't be drunk with wine, because that will ruin your life. Instead, let the Holy Spirit fill and control you" (Eph. 5:18). Paul describes this kind of living in this way: "If we are living now by the Holy Spirit, let us follow the Holy Spirit's leading in every part of our lives" (Gal. 5:25).

Perhaps right now you are saying, "I can't do this! Living by faith sounds too hard. I get up early every morning and start my day at full throttle. I have to get the kids ready for school, get myself ready for work and get everyone into the car before 7:30. And that's the slow part of my day! My work schedule is exhausting. But at the same time, part of me is worried about how the kids are doing where they are. By the time I pick them up, throw something on for supper, and clean up the dishes, I'm irritable. And I still have several more chores to do before I can slow down. How am I going to fit living a life of faith into my schedule?"

That's the exciting part of a living faith. You don't add it to your life; it is the source of your life. Just as the sap runs effortlessly through the maple tree, the Holy Spirit's power is always available to you.

To have a living faith, practice what Bill and I like to call "spiritual breathing." When you breathe physically, you exhale the impure air and inhale the pure. Exhaling the impure spiritually means confessing all known sin to God. John writes, "If we confess our sins to [God], he is faithful and just to forgive us and to cleanse us from every wrong" (1 John 1:9).

Then we inhale the pure by asking God to fill us with His Holy Spirit (see Eph. 5:18).

It's that simple. You can do it while you're in the shower, as you're pouring cereal into bowls, when you get behind the wheel, as you mediate that argument between your teenagers. Begin your day by asking God to fill you with His Spirit. Then each time you find yourself entangled in sin, sporting a bad attitude or in the need of the Spirit's power, practice spiritual breathing. You will be amazed at how much God can do through you when you give the Spirit moment-by-moment control of your life. That's real living by faith!

Faith and Good Works

This brings up another issue related to living faith. What is the relationship between faith and good works? Many people are confused about this. What about people who say they have faith but don't show it? What about times when I do the right thing but my actions are just mechanical, without faith? James writes about this in his book:

> Dear brothers and sisters, what's the use of saying you have faith if you don't prove it by your actions? That kind of faith can't save anyone. Suppose you see a brother or sister who needs food or clothing, and you say, "Well, good-bye and God bless you; stay warm and eat well"—but then you don't give that person any food or clothing. What good does that do? So you see, it isn't enough just to have faith. Faith that doesn't show itself by good deeds is no faith at all—it is dead and useless. Now, someone may argue, "Some people have faith; others have good deeds." I say, "I can't see your faith if you don't have good deeds, but I will show you my faith through my good deeds" (Jas. 2:14-18).

James is giving us criteria for recognizing living faith. Let's look at both sides of the faith/good deeds issue.

Faith Without Good Works

When you first became a believer, what was your reaction? For most people, they wanted to tell everyone what God did for them. They expressed their faith through their actions. The good works were proof that their faith was living and growing. The good works didn't produce the faith, but the faith produced the good works.

When a branch is connected to the vine, it produces green leaves naturally. Anyone looking at it can tell it is vitally connected to the vine. In the same way, our good works show the world that we are connected to Jesus Christ.

In reverse, you could glue a healthy branch onto a trunk and the inevitable would occur. The branch would wither. It wasn't really connected to the vine. So you can't fake that faith connection. Only the Holy Spirit can produce a living faith that results in true good works.

Good Works Without Faith

Have you ever known a "good" person who did the right thing but had no faith in God? Unbelievers can do moral actions, but they cannot perform good deeds that spring from a living faith. Even more so, as believers we can participate in "good things," but unless our power comes from the Holy Spirit, they are not good deeds in God's eyes. Good deeds result from a living faith.

That difference describes the before-and-after results of my life when I struggled with dissatisfaction in the early days of Bill's and my ministry. In our Bel Air mansion, I was performing many ministry functions, such as preparing the house for meetings, raising my boys in a godly manner, being a good wife to Bill. But I was doing all this in my own strength, not out of faith. I was not walking in the power of the Holy Spirit. That's why I became so dissatisfied and unhappy. But when I turned my roles and problems in managing all my tasks over to the Lord, I began working under the Spirit's control. What a difference! My faith that God could overcome my difficulties produced true good deeds in my life. As I explained earlier, the Lord then began to use me—even in ways I hadn't expected. That's living faith!

Living Faith in the Big Moments of Life

I consider that time when I turned my schedule over to God as a big moment of faith in my life. It set a precedent for how I would handle many more years of busy mothering, working in the ministry, traveling and so many other pressures. If I hadn't made that decision then, I would have hampered both Bill's and my life from then on. After my decision, I could look back to that moment whenever I needed to rearrange my attitudes in the future and reaffirm my commitment to walking in the Spirit in my daily living.

I could give you so many other examples of big moments of faith that changed the course of the person involved. God has a way of revealing to us what He wants us to do. But I want to tell you of an incident in the life of President Ronald Reagan that shows just how God works.

I came to know President Reagan when I was co-chair of the National Day of Prayer Task Force. I found that President Reagan had a deep faith that was influenced by the life of his godly mother. He was responsible for helping set a permanent day for the National Day of Prayer on the National Calendar.

On March 30, 1981, just 70 days into his presidency, an assassin penetrated the ring of secret service agents around him and fired several bullets toward the president. One of the bullets ricocheted off the President's limousine and hit him in the chest. Immediately, he was rushed to the emergency room.

During surgery, the doctors removed the bullet, which was nestled against his left lung only half an inch from his beating heart. The bullet was sent to the FBI lab, which found that it was a special type called a "Devastator." It was made to flatten out on entry to the body to cause extra damage, and its tip was filled with a toxic poison. For some reason, the tip did not explode on impact with the president's body.

President Reagan firmly believed that God had spared his life for a purpose. He believed he was supposed to fulfill some mission with the rest of his life. He wrote in his diary, "Whatever happens now, I owe my life to God and will try to serve him in every way I can."[2]

President Reagan's crisis that day provided him with a living faith that enabled him to handle the conflict with the Soviet Union with the utmost wisdom and steadfastness. Because of his tough stance, the Berlin Wall fell and freedom spread across Eastern Europe!

You, too, will experience those big moments in your life. They are turning points, and they will set the course for living by faith if you follow the Spirit's leading and the principles in God's Word about abiding in Him. If you fail to act on faith through the big moments, however, they can become stumbling points in your life. Just imagine what might have happened if President Reagan had said after he was shot, "This job's too tough. I'm just staying in the White House until my term is over." That's why we must trust God for His control and leave the results to Him. We obey Him during these big moments of faith so that we bring glory to Him and accomplish what He has planned for us through them.

Living Faith and Your Life Attitudes

Walking in the Spirit means more than handling those big decisions through faith. Our life attitudes must also be centered in our living faith—day by day. Otherwise, we face disaster.

Each family lives its life differently, and each woman deals with her personality in her own way. Unfortunately, some women have opted for some ineffective ways of handling bad attitudes. No matter what stage or age your family is, you have the responsibility to live out your faith in a way that brings honor and glory to God. Paul said it well in 2 Corinthians 1:24:

> But that does not mean we want to tell you exactly how to put your faith into practice. We want to work together with you so you will be full of joy as you stand firm in your faith.

We will live tragic lives if we fail to stand firm in our faith, keeping our attitudes in check under the power of the Holy Spirit. God's way is the only way, but it is so easy to let our attitudes step into sin. One woman's description of her life's attitudes echoes that of many—dissatisfaction. My heart was saddened when she told me this:

> As a child, I thought when I got to high school that would be the "ultimate." There I would find happiness. When I got to high school, I thought surely the great joy of life comes in college. But when I got to college, it seemed happiness would not come until I got in the right sorority. After joining the "best house," I determined genuine satisfaction was only possible when I found the right man to marry. But after the wedding, my desire for fulfillment centered in living in the right house in the right section of the city. After moving into our new home, I looked forward to having a child and being fulfilled as a mother. The day the baby was christened, we had an extravagant party at our house. After the guests had left, I thought, *Now where else can I go for the fulfillment which continues to elude me?* A few years later I separated from my husband and we were divorced, and I began to realize there was no place to go.

This woman couldn't see that her only hope was faith in Christ. Whether we look to major events or material pleasures of life to give us a sense of purpose and fulfillment, we will find ourselves still unsatisfied. A friend tells the story of a woman who came to her for counseling. She was struggling with an attitude of materialism. She believed that having a new stove would help her find satisfaction at home. To please her, her husband saved his money and bought her a stove for Christmas. Absolutely delighted, she thought, *I can bake all I want and everything will turn out all right.*

After three weeks, she discovered the refrigerator wasn't functioning properly and she couldn't store the things she was baking. When she discussed the problem with her husband, he consented to buy a new refrigerator on time payments.

As they enjoyed their new stove and refrigerator, they noticed how shabby the kitchen looked. So they splurged again and re-decorated the kitchen.

In the course of entertaining, they would bring their guests into the prettiest room in the house—the kitchen. However, they did not want to entertain their guests in the kitchen, so they decided to redo their living room and make it as nice as the kitchen.

Soon their interior decorating went from the living room to the bedrooms until their whole house was completely refurbished. Finally, after a few months, their home was beautiful, but they didn't have ten cents to spare to purchase an ice-cream cone.

The price of their extravagances took its toll not only on their pocketbook but also on their relationship. Although they did not realize what had happened because of their strained finances, they were soon at each other's throats and in a psychologist's office asking, "What's gone wrong with our marriage?"

Having an abundance of money won't solve attitude problems, either. I have known individuals who have said, "I cannot understand why people who have money are not happy." And yet, some of the most miserable people are those who have money—a lot of money.

On the other hand, I know some who go to the other extreme and say, "I would be happy if I didn't have anything." One woman I know gives everything away except a meager amount on which to live, because she believes people who have less money are happier. She reached that conclusion because she doesn't know anyone in her affluent station of life that is happy.

Other women try to find fulfillment by serving in a philanthropic organization or helping deprived individuals. It's wonderful to be able to have the time, finances, energy and possibly even prestige and influence to exert for needy organizations. But when this is our only avenue to contentment, it too brings emptiness, frustration and dissatisfaction. The only solution to problems of the spirit is living by faith and trusting God.

Each of us has areas of our life with which we will always struggle. I'd like to tell you that today I never feel frustrated about having too many responsibilities in the home! But I sometimes still have to reaffirm that God is in control of my daily schedule.

Perhaps you are dogged with feelings of depression. This can become a life attitude when not dealt with in the power of the Holy Spirit. You may not be able to point to a time when you decided to become depressed, because it crept up on you so gradually. What about a critical spirit? Is that your weakness? Or an irritable temper? We can become entangled in so many wrong attitudes. Sometimes, we may not even recognize when we hurt others or become insensitive to God's Spirit.

This is why walking in the Spirit by consistently practicing spiritual breathing is so essential to a living faith. Another step we can take is to periodically search our attitudes by praying Psalm 139:23 to God: "Search me, O God, and know my heart; test me and know my thoughts." As you quietly meditate on God and this verse, He will reveal your wrong attitudes to you.

Now that you have dealt with the big moments in your life and the problem attitudes that have been thwarting your satisfaction, you may think that you have encountered the majority of barriers to living a vibrant faith. But what about those small moments that you tend to push aside because they don't seem too important? Small moments can sometimes become big moments if left to fester.

Living Faith and the Small Moments of Faith

How do you treat your family when you are tired and you are behind closed doors? Do you act out of faith or in your own human strength?

What is your temperament when you get out of bed in the morning? Does the sun come up in your eyes or are you stormy?

How do you address those mood swings that come now and then? Can you rise above them or do they get you down?

How do you handle those small irritations at work? Do you avoid the coworker who said ugly things about you once? What about the colleague who shirks her fair share of the work? The boss who plays favorites?

Walking in the Spirit can turn everyday problems into moments of faith. Rather than becoming discouraged or disgruntled, we can let these situations stretch us to become more like Jesus.

We become patient when we're short tempered.

We become cool-headed when our emotions threaten to erupt.

We use wisdom when our brain is frozen in fear.

We can laugh through our tears.

We can hug instead of blame.

We can do these things because we turn to God instead of to our egos.

I appreciate the way that Paul puts our responsibility: "Be on guard. Stand true to what you believe. Be courageous. Be strong. And everything you do must be done with love" (1 Cor. 16:13). Isn't that a description of living those small moments in faith?

Abraham, that great man of faith, is commended in James 2:21-24:

Don't you remember that our ancestor Abraham was declared right with God because of what he did when he offered his son Isaac on the altar? You see, he was trusting God so much that he was willing to do whatever God told him to do. His faith was made complete by what he did—by his actions. And so it happened just as the Scriptures say: "Abraham believed God, so God declared him to be righteous." He was even called "the friend of God." So you see, we are made right with God by what we do, not by faith alone.

Do you have that kind of living faith? Are your good deeds only for show, like those cathedrals turned into museums? Or have you joined the "army of worms" who are marching ahead for Christ's kingdom? Here are some small faith moments you may experience with your new attitude:

- You send up a prayer for strength and answer gently when your teenager asks another off-the-wall question.

- You recall a Bible verse on love rather than retaliating when your neighbor spills his garbage on your lawn again.

- You practice spiritual breathing when someone cuts you off on the freeway.
- You thank God for your family as you do that huge pile of dishes.
- You praise God for His creation wonders instead of getting mad that the rain has ruined your plans for a picnic.
- You give God the credit for your beautiful house when a friend compliments you instead of letting her comments puff up your pride.

That's what we do. We live by faith in every small moment, and then they don't turn into big, ugly scenes that hurt others.

Our living faith will naturally lead us into another facet of our faith—a loving faith. This was something that our wonderful Lord Jesus exemplified so well when He walked on this earth. It becomes an exciting stepping-stone in our journey toward the realization of our faith—our reunion in heaven with Him.

A Pathway to Deepen My Faith

1. Learning from the Chapter
Read Galatians 2:20. How does this verse describe living in faith?

_____

_____

_____

_____

Look up John 15:1-5. In your own words, describe the importance of Jesus as the vine and you as the branch as given in these verses.

_____

_____

_____

_____

How have you seen this principle work in your life?

_____

_____

_____

_____

_____

What small moment of faith have you experienced since beginning this book? What did it do for your spiritual life?

_____

_____

_____

_____

2. Knowing God's Word

Another aspect of a living faith is that we will bear fruit. How does that relate to the idea of the Vine and the branches?

_____

_____

_____

_____

Read the following verses, and then write down what they say about being spiritually fruitful.

Galatians 5:22

_____

_____

_____

_____

Colossians 1:10

_____

_____

_____

_____

James 3:18

_____
_____
_____
_____

3. Applying God's Word
Read once again the verses that explain spiritual breathing:

1 John 1:9—Exhaling

_____
_____
_____
_____

Ephesians 5:18—Inhaling

_____
_____
_____
_____

Psalm 139:23—Meditating

_____
_____
_____
_____

Practice spiritual breathing today as you complete your tasks. Then begin your new day by using spiritual breathing again.

Notes
1. Paul Hattaway, Brother Yun, Peter Xu Yongze, and Enoch Wang, *Back to Jerusalem: Three Chinese House Church Leaders Share Their Vision to Complete the Great Commission* (Waynesboro, GA: Gabriel Publishing, 2003), p. 91.
2. Mary Beth Brown, *Hand of Providence: The Strong and Quiet Faith of Ronald Reagan* (Nashville, TN: Thomas Nelson Books, 2004), pp. 1-16.

5

A Loving Faith

You love God as much as the one you love the least.
JOHN J. HUGO

Have you ever noticed what happens to retail advertising at the beginning of February? Engagement ring commercials pop up everywhere—on TV, in newspaper ads, on billboards and on the radio. The theme running through most of these ads is that the beauty of a diamond expresses an undying love between a man and a woman.

Where did the connection between diamonds and love originate? The ancient Egyptians had a fascinating theory about love. They believed that the *vena amores*, translated as the "vein of love," flowed directly from the heart to the third finger of the left hand. That corresponds to what we call the ring finger. The Greeks, on the other hand, were entranced with the beauty of diamonds. They had a tradition that said that the glow from this most dazzling gemstone reflected the eternal flame of love.

When the Egyptian and Greek myths were combined, the result was the diamond engagement ring. In 1477, Archduke Maximilian of Austria presented the first engagement ring to Mary of Burgundy. He began a tradition that has since spread throughout the world.

I'm sure you will agree with me that love is a powerful force. A young couple that wants to spend the rest of their lives together will conquer mountains of hardships to be with each other. What do you do in your life that is motivated by love? If you have children, I'm sure you can name countless things you do for them just because you love them. We do the same for our parents, husbands, friends and sometimes even for people we don't know.

A story in the newspaper recently illustrates how people will help others they don't even know out of love for their fellow man. A group in Iraq is trying to help other Iraqis reconstruct their lives. From 1994 to 2001, Saddam Hussein, sadistic dictator of that country, ordered his minions to perform all kinds of abuse on his own countrymen. One technique he instituted was cutting off the ear of any soldier caught deserting his post in the army. Anyone with a mutilated ear was shunned in Iraqi society. These people were not allowed by law to have a job, and most never married because of the humiliation they constantly suffered. Saad Mohammed Allwan was an Iraqi soldier who refused to fight against his own Kurdish countrymen in northern Iraq and therefore was given this punishment. He says of his life after 1994, "Sometimes I would have preferred to die."

Some Iraqi physicians and others formed a group called the National Iraqi Association for the Defense of Human Rights for the purpose of helping people like Saad. Through this group, hundreds of people are receiving plastic surgery to repair the damage they suffered.

One man whose life has been drastically changed because of this reconstructive ear surgery says, "It feels so good to be able to walk around in the street again and not be embarrassed or feel like people are looking at you." The love of these Iraqi volunteers has helped many rebuild their lives.

We can see expressions of love in so many places around us. Loving people volunteer at soup kitchens, serve as foster parents, coach handicap sports teams, help build homes for the poor or take care of the needs of an elderly neighbor. Their actions warm our hearts.

But there is a kind of love that is more powerful than any other—God's love. As humans, our love is fickle and conditional. We are tempted to withhold our love when someone hurts us. Some people will only love people who fit a certain ethnic or class criteria. Others will only love if they are loved first. But God's love is different. We have all experienced His gentleness, compassion, forgiveness, mercy and patience. They are all components of His inexhaustible love.

The New Testament was written in Greek, a language that uses a specific word when talking about God's kind of love. Called *agape*, it is defined as a supernatural, unconditional love that is expressed as an act of God's will, not merely as a feeling. This love is given freely, not because the person receiving the love has earned it, but because of who God is. God loves because of His holy character rather than because we are worthy of His love. Sometimes, God's love is "in spite of" rather than "because of."

We have seen the greatest example of *agape* love—when Jesus Christ died on the cross for our sins. None of us deserved or earned that love. Jesus gave of Himself freely. No one can measure the length, depth or breadth of God's love, because it is limitless. We will never exhaust it. In fact, it is richer and greater than we could ever imagine.

The power of God's love is so much greater than any love a human can have on his own. Let me illustrate with an example.

One day, a first-grade teacher explained to her friend how much she loved the 20 students in her class. They were her pride and joy. She felt like she was just filled with love for them.

At the end of the year, the teacher and her husband found out that they could adopt a baby in a few weeks. Their little girl was born just a few days after the first-grade class matriculated into second grade and the summer break began. One day, a social worker placed the tiny baby into her arms.

One thought amazed the teacher. As she held that little person and the baby squirmed in her arms, she realized that the love she had developed for her students after teaching them for an entire school year didn't compare to the love she had for this baby girl who had only been in her arms for a few moments!

Of course, we all understand how God planted a special love between a mother and her child. But the comparison illustrates this truth: The love we have for people when we love with God's love is way beyond the love we have when we love in our human strength. God's love is so far above any other kind of love that we cannot put it on the same plane as any other. His love has special power and endurance, depth and strength. In our own strength, we can love people and even perform great deeds for them, like the physicians in Iraq or the volunteers in Habitat for Humanity. But any love we muster up on our own is like a vapor compared to the love we will have when we let God love through us. Then we, too, will be spreading *agape*—unconditional love.

But how do we love people with God's love? Let's admit it; some people are difficult to love! We do so by loving by faith. And faith comes from God. I'll explain more about loving by faith in the rest of this chapter. But simply know that this simple act of faith will transform our relationships and give us incredible joy!

Because God never changes, we can be sure that what He says about His love will never change either. God says, "I am the Lord, and I do not change" (Mal. 3:6).

In 1 Corinthians 13:4-7, the apostle Paul gives us God's description of God's love.

> Love is patient and kind. Love is not jealous or boastful or proud or rude. Love does not demand its own way. Love is not irritable, and it keeps no record of when it has been wronged. It is never glad about injustice but rejoices whenever the truth wins out. Love never gives up, never loses faith, is always hopeful, and endures through every circumstance.

This is the kind of love that God shows us. Does this give you a feeling of deep security and comfort in placing your life in His hands? Through love, He is always looking out for our best.

For years, Bill and I taught about the concept we call loving by faith. This kind of spiritual love will transform the way you relate to people and how God can use you in His kingdom. To understand loving by faith, we must learn the basics about God's love. We can count on five truths that underlie the love that God has for us. The first truth about love is that He loves us unconditionally.

God Loves Us Unconditionally

Have you ever read the parable of the prodigal son that Jesus told the people of His day? It is found in Luke 15:11-32. A father had two sons, one who was compliant and one who was rebellious. The rebellious son took his share of the inheritance, ran off and began to party. He attracted all kinds of friends. But within a short period of time, he had run through his money and all his "friends" deserted him. When the economy in the area plunged, the only job the son could find was slopping hogs on a farm. He was so desperately poor by this time that he stooped to eating the pigs' food.

One day as he was fighting the pigs for food, he said to himself, "What am I doing here? Even the lowliest hired man on my father's estate has more than enough to eat. I'm going home, beg my father for his forgiveness, and ask him to give me any job he would pass my way" (see Luke 15:17-19).

What the rebellious son didn't realize was that all this time his father had been watching for him to return home. The father had forgiven his son long ago. When the father saw his son coming far down the road, he ran to hug him. He ordered his servants to prepare a huge party to celebrate the homecoming of his once-lost son.

The father in this story represents God, our heavenly Father. He loved us long before we came to Him in faith. He loves us through our weaknesses and even in our sin. Paul writes about the depth of God's love:

> I am convinced that nothing can ever separate us from his love. Death can't, and life can't. The angels can't, and the demons can't. Our fears for today, our worries about tomorrow, and even the powers of hell can't keep God's love away. Whether we are high above the sky or in the deepest ocean, nothing in all creation will ever be able to separate us from the love of God that is revealed in Christ Jesus our Lord (Rom. 8:38-39).

What greater assurance can we have about the limitless length, breadth and depth of God's love? It is unconditional and will never change, no matter what we do. It is the rock we can stand on. Whenever we feel hurt, lonely, afraid or friendless, we can count on God's love to sustain us. Because we can be so sure of God's love in our life, we can obey the second truth about love.

We Are Commanded to Love

If someone were to ask you, "What's the most important command in the Bible?" what would you answer? Would you pick one of the Ten Commandments? One of the beatitudes that Jesus gave in His famous Sermon on the Mount?

One day, someone asked Jesus that very question. Here is His answer:

> "You must love the Lord your God with all your heart, all your soul, and all your mind." This is the first and greatest commandment. A second is equally important: "Love your neighbor as yourself." All the other commandments and all the demands of the prophets are based on these two commandments (Matt. 22:37-40).

Does it surprise you that Jesus placed such a high priority on love? It shouldn't amaze us, because He demonstrated His love so clearly to us by dying for us.

In fact, in those verses, Jesus taught that all the other commandments in the Bible are related to love. We don't steal, because we love others and don't want to hurt them. We don't lie, because we love others so much that we want to be forthcoming with them. And of course we don't want to break any of God's laws, because we love Him so much. Therefore, we must take Jesus' command to love very seriously. Love for God first, then for others, should underlie our motivation in all we do. We should love God and others just like God loves us—unconditionally.

But how can we do this? I'll have to admit that I've met some prickly people who I'd prefer to avoid. I have had people in my life who have opposed me and what I stand for, and they have done this in hurtful ways. Believe me, I found it almost impossible to love some people!

On the other hand, I have found a resource that allows me to love even my enemies. He is the Holy Spirit. Paul writes, "We know how dearly God loves us, because he has given us the Holy Spirit to fill our hearts with his love" (Rom. 5:5). I don't have to love these people! The Holy Spirit has come to love them through me! That means that I don't have to depend on myself to love—I can depend on the Holy Spirit to do it through me. *That's the essence of loving by faith.*

This spiritual principle is so freeing to me! God loves me; I love Him back. He produces love in my heart, which I spread to other people. And Jesus even gives me a measurement to tell if I'm displaying enough love. He said, "I command you to love each other in the same way that I love you" (John 15:12). Just think of how much love that is! He's going to pour love into my life so that I can give it to others.

This kind of love is like the most beautiful wardrobe you could ever purchase. The designer ensembles are waiting in your closet for you to enjoy. Will you put them on? This is how Paul describes what you'll be doing: "The most important piece of clothing you must wear is love. Love is what binds us all together in perfect harmony" (Col. 3:14). How is your wardrobe today? Are you putting on the love of God?

These commands lead us to the next truth about love, which we have already begun to discover.

We Cannot Love in Our Own Strength

Lisa was a supervisor in the county offices. In her building, she noticed one young male employee who didn't get along with any of the supervisors. He was originally from the Middle East, and he consistently came in late for work, left early and came back a half hour late after lunch. All the supervisors hated dealing with this man because it took so much of their time to manage what he was or was not doing.

One day when Lisa came to work, she was called into her manager's office. "Lisa," the woman informed her, "I'm transferring this young man into your department."

Lisa went back to her desk and fumed. *My manager keeps dumping the most difficult problems on me. Why does she give me the employee no one else can handle?* Her attitude was so evident that the entire office knew how she felt.

From that day on, Lisa's problems multiplied. The young man began exhibiting the same bad habits in Lisa's unit that he had shown in other departments. He caused so many headaches for her that she just couldn't stand him.

But the Lord began convicting Lisa of her unloving attitude. She began pleading with Him, "Please help me resolve my bad attitude toward this employee."

But she found it impossible to love him. She'd have to take a walk every day during her morning break to pray for him and about her attitude. Then she'd have to do this all over again during her afternoon break because her attitude had already deteriorated.

Finally one day she realized that the Lord had begun to give her a love for this young man. She was shocked because she knew she could never have loved him on her own!

Gradually, she and the young man developed a warm relationship. They had some heart-to-heart talks in which Lisa was able to share her faith in Christ with him. Eventually, he became one of her best employees.

One day, he came over to her desk and said, "You don't know how much I appreciate the fact that you care about me. None of the other supervisors cared enough to force me to achieve excellence. You were the only one." His words touched Lisa deeply.

Some time later, Lisa was reassigned to another position in the county in an office some miles away. The first person to e-mail her in her new office and encourage her was this young man.

When we encounter difficult people to love, or when the people whom we love are difficult, God will do the loving through us. As Lisa realized, we can't love on our own. And although we won't always see the kinds of results that Lisa experienced, God will produce miracles in our life. This will come from our next truth.

We Can Love with God's Love

The Holy Spirit is our key to living with God's love. Galatians 5:22-23 says, "When the Holy Spirit controls our lives, he will produce this kind of fruit in us: love, joy, peace, patience, kindness, goodness, faithfulness, gentleness, and self-control."

Did you notice that "love" heads the list of all these qualities? If you think about it, none of them can be produced without love.

It's when love fills our hearts that we have joy.

Love helps us to have peace with God and with each other.

Patience is only possible through love for others.

Kindness is a product of love.

When we love, our attitude naturally reflects goodness.

Love keeps us faithful when we want to quit.

A loving person is gentle with those she loves.

Because love considers the other person first, we are able to control our own actions.

Producing the fruit of the Spirit brings us back to walking in the Spirit by continuously practicing spiritual breathing. God gives us the love. He also gives us the motivation to love. He gives us the ability to love. Without Him, we can produce certain acts of love, but we will never be able to love with His unconditional love. He abundantly provides us with His *agape* love to share with others.

That leads us to the final truth about love.

We Can Love by Faith

By now, are you getting the idea of how to love by faith? Even though we can take steps to love by faith, it remains a miraculous work of God in our hearts. But God is always willing to give us more than enough love for any situation or person we encounter.

In a little book called *How You Can Love by Faith*, my husband wrote a clear description of what it means to love by faith:

Everything about the Christian life is based on faith. You love by faith just as you received Christ by faith, just as you are filled with the Holy Spirit by faith, and just as you walk by faith.[1]

Hebrews 11:6 says, "It is impossible to please God without faith." Obviously there will be no demonstration of God's love where there is no faith.

If you have difficulty loving others, remember that Jesus has commanded, "Love each other just as much as I love you" (John 13:34, *TLB*). It is God's will for you to love. He would not command you to do something that He will not enable you to do. In 1 John 5:14-15, God promises that if you ask anything according to His will, He hears and answers you. Relating this promise to God's command, you can claim by faith the privilege of loving with His love.

God has an unending supply of His divine, supernatural *agape* love for you. It is for you to claim, to grow on, to spread to others and thus to reach hundreds and thousands with the love that counts, the love that will bring them to Jesus Christ.

In order to experience and share this love, you must claim it by faith; that is, trust His promise that He will give you all that you need to do His will on the basis of His command and promise.

I have practiced loving by faith for many years, and it works. Let me give you three simple steps that help me understand when I should love by faith.

Listen to God's Spirit. He will produce compassion in your heart for people He wants you to especially love. That feeling inside you for other people is God's compassion streaming through you to them. He may give you a burden for that unlovable child in the neighborhood or that blatantly immoral woman across the street. He may lead you to show love to a critical relative or a belligerent colleague. Ask God to lay someone on your heart that you can love by faith. When the Lord reveals these people to you, begin praying for them and ministering to them.

Make a list of people who rub you the wrong way. Do you have any enemies? Do you feel hostile toward certain people? Has someone let you down? Do you have an abusive parent? Write down the names of these people and begin to pray for them. Expect God to work through you. You may just see changed lives—especially your own!

Pray for each person God wants you to love by faith. Prayer changes attitudes. It's like the catalyst that opens up your heart to loving with God's love. Be specific in your prayers. How hard it is to harbor a grudge against someone when you are praying for that person's welfare!

When you take these steps, you will be amazed at what God leads you to do. Sometimes the actions you take will have to be a moment-by-moment act of faith. Other times, God will produce so much love in your life that you will feel exhilarated. Either way, you will be obeying God's greatest command—to love others.

The Perfect Wedding

When the engagement finally leads to a wedding, what a celebration of joy! Everyone who is in the presence of the bride and groom experiences their excitement.

I like to think of loving by faith as a marriage of two of God's most precious gifts—faith and love. What joy we will experience! With faith, we have great hope for the future. With love, we maximize the journey!

Today, God is bringing back to our remembrance the biblical wedding of the two. Through faith, that supernatural divine love of God will reach out where nothing else can capture men and women for Christ. The love that results from that faith will captivate people everywhere so that as we live and love by faith, we will spread God's love throughout the world. This love is contagious, attractive and aggressive. It creates hunger for God. It is active—constantly looking for loving things to do, people to uplift, lives to change. Miracles will happen where God's love takes root in faith.

Charles Colson tells a story of a miracle of love and faith that happened during World War II. Jacob DeShazer, sergeant in the armed forces, was enraged when he learned about the attack on Pearl Harbor. He wanted to exact revenge on the Japanese.

In 1942, he got his chance. He was a bombardier with Doolittle's Raiders, who attacked Tokyo. Tragically, his plane ran out of fuel, and he and the other crew members became Japanese POWs. For 40 months, he endured the most inhumane conditions, including 30 months of solitary confinement. During this time, three of his buddies were executed and one died of slow starvation.

Under these conditions, the natural result would be that DeShazer's hatred would grow exponentially. Instead, he got hold of a Bible and began reading it. Soon, he received Christ as his Savior, and his bitter heart began to melt. The account of Jesus forgiving His executioners from the cross became real to him. He decided that God wanted him to love his tormentors with God's love.

In 1945, paratroopers liberated the camp where DeShazer was imprisoned. In time, the story of his testimony was printed in a little pamphlet called "I Was a Prisoner of Japan."

But this isn't the end of this inspiring story. Another man was also deeply affected by the war. Japanese Navy pilot Mitsuo Fuchida was Chief Commander during the attack on Pearl Harbor. During the remainder of the war, he chalked up 10,000 combat hours against the Allies. Miraculously, he escaped death in the bombing of Hiroshima when he was called away out of the city one day before the atomic bombs were dropped.

After the war, he went back to his farm on Osaka demoralized and discouraged. One day, as he disembarked from a train, he saw an American distributing literature. He took the pamphlet. The title? "I Was a Prisoner of Japan." It was DeShazer's testimony!

Fuchida read the pamphlet. He says, "His story . . . was something I could not explain. . . . The peaceful motivation I had read about was exactly what I was seeking. Since the American had found it in the Bible, I decided to purchase one myself. . . .

"I read . . . the prayer of Jesus Christ at His death: 'Father, forgive them; for they know not what they do' (Luke 23:34, *KJV*). I was impressed that I was certainly one of those for whom He had prayed. The many men I had killed had been slaughtered in the name of patriotism, for I did not understand the love that Christ wishes to implant within every heart.

"Right at that moment, I seemed to meet Jesus for the first time.... I requested Him to forgive my sins and change me from a bitter, disillusioned ex-pilot into a well-balanced Christian with purpose in living."

What is so miraculous about this story is that Captain Fuchida and Sergeant DeShazer met and even spent some time sharing their testimonies in front of the Japanese people. For 30 years, both together and separately, they helped tell thousands of people about the love of Jesus.

Who else could have turned bitter enemies into partners? Only God. As we understand the true nature of God's love, we can't help but spread it through our faith.

Once we know God and the power of His love, we will also want to develop another facet of our faith—serving faith. As we add each of these beautiful facets of faith, our lives begin to reflect more clearly the wonderful nature of our God!

A Pathway to Deepen My Faith

1. Learning from the Chapter
Who are the most difficult people to love in your life?

_____
_____
_____
_____

2. Knowing God's Word
Study the "love" that Paul describes in 1 Corinthians 13. What surprises you most about God's definition of love?

_____
_____
_____
_____

How does this love picture the life of Christ?

_____

_____

_____

_____

_____

_____

_____

What one verse in the 1 Corinthians passage do you need to apply
most in your life?

_____

_____

_____

_____

_____

_____

3. Applying God's Word

To apply loving by faith, first read each of these verses and then
write them in your own words.

Hebrews 11:6

_____

_____

_____

_____

_____

John 13:34

_____

_____

_____

_____

_____

1 John 5:14-15

_____
_____
_____
_____
_____

Then practice loving by faith. The following three steps will help
you get started:

1. Listen to God's Spirit.
2. Make a list of people who rub you the wrong way.
3. Pray for each person God wants you to love by faith.

Note
1. Bill Bright, *How You Can Love by Faith (Transferable Concepts)* (Orlando, FL: New Life
Publications, 1998), p. 20.

6

A Serving Faith

*In the kingdom of God, service is not a stepping-stone to nobility:
it is nobility, the only kind of nobility that is recognized.*

T. W. MANSON

I want you to imagine with me that you were in the room with Jesus when He washed the disciples' feet. He took a towel, wrapped it around Himself, filled a basin with water and knelt before one of the disciples. What if you had been one of those disciples? What would you have thought? What would you have said? How would you have felt?

Jesus dips His towel into the water and then begins wiping your feet with His hands. The roughness of the towel, the coolness of the water, the gentleness of the Master's fingers fill your senses. Would you have felt ashamed that He, the Ruler of the universe, the King of kings, was stooping before you? Would you have been conscious of every piece of dirt on your toes?

That moment was one of the most awesome events in the lives of the disciples. They had walked with Jesus for three years up to that time. They had seen Him heal the sick and raise the dead. They had heard Him preach unbelievably wise sermons. And here He was, washing their feet!

Of course, Jesus was teaching His disciples one of the greatest lessons of Christianity—that the servant heart is the one God desires. Jesus displayed His servant heart by agreeing to go to the cross for our sake. He didn't have to go, but He did. He endured for us what we could not pay for ourselves because of our sin.

What does this show you about Jesus? How does this compare with the world's view of what a leader does?

I'm amazed at how the world thinks. If you are a leader in the world's opinion, you deserve special treatment and honor. You are given special privileges. Then the world howls when the leaders to whom they have given so much power abuse their advantages and take money and power for themselves. I think of the Food for Iraq scandal that hit the news some time ago. Many of the highest personnel in the United Nations were implicated in taking billions of dollars from the Iraqi people, who have little or nothing. These UN leaders assumed their positions in a noble goal to help the people of the world live better lives. Yet these same leaders deprived the poorest of people of what was actually theirs in the first place—the profits from their own oil. Now the news media was screaming "foul play" and the UN officials ran to cover up their sins. Truly, the adulation and privilege showered upon leaders in the world only results in sinful humans taking advantage of their fellow man.

This is why having a servant faith is so necessary. Jesus knew that to be great, a person must be a servant first. That's the example He showed us while He was on earth. He laid aside His glory and assumed the role of a servant. He even accepted the excruciating death of the cross. Later, when God says that the time is right, the Father will crown the Son and announce His glory to the world. But for the time that He was on earth, Jesus laid aside His glory and assumed the role of a servant.

The story of Jesus washing the feet of the disciples can be found in John 13:1-17. In verses 12-17, Jesus tells His disciples why He gave them this example:

> Do you understand what I was doing? You call me "Teacher" and "Lord," and you are right, because it is true. And since I, the Lord and Teacher, have washed your feet, you ought to wash each other's feet. I have given you an example to follow. Do as I have done to you. How true it is that a servant is not greater than the master. Nor are messengers more important than the one who sends them. You know these things—now do them! That is the path of blessing.

Since our faith is the evidence of what we cannot see, and what we do not see and hope to see is Jesus, we serve in faith, anticipating our meeting with Him face to face. We obey His command to follow His example and serve others.

This is the spirit of the gospel that impelled Bill and me to do something strategic early in our ministry. We wrote a contract in which we dedicated ourselves to be slaves of Jesus Christ. That particular Sunday morning, we had an argument about Bill's insensitivity to me during one of his counseling sessions. After the church services, he had left me sitting in the car for hours in the hot church parking lot. I didn't know where he was or what he was doing. He did not intentionally forget about my welfare, but in the moment of helping someone else, he forgot about my needs. Later that afternoon, we talked through our problem, and then we decided that we needed to write down our goals in life to better understand each other.

Bill went to one part of the house and I went to another. We both wrote down our goals and then met to compare our lists. Although my list was more practical and Bill's was more visionary, we both wanted the same thing—to serve God with all our heart. That led us to write a contract in which we gave ourselves to God completely. We signed the contract to symbolize the intent of our hearts. This was one of the biggest moments of faith in our lives.

That contract meant so much to us over the years. As you can well imagine, we had our ups and downs in the ministry, our trials and successes. We had disagreements with other staff members and times when finances were stretched to the limit. But no matter what happened, that commitment of giving ourselves to God as slaves of Jesus Christ kept our focus on the mission we had chosen. Neither Bill nor I ever regretted making that choice.

Being a slave of Jesus Christ is what serving faith is all about. A slave has no personal rights, no desires to build his own kingdom; he or she is always seeking to work for the master's benefit. The apostle Paul, who gave himself totally to the work of God, declared himself to be a slave of Jesus Christ. At the beginning of his letter to the church in Rome, he writes, "This letter is from Paul,

Jesus Christ's slave, chosen by God to be an apostle and sent out to preach his Good News" (Rom. 1:1). Paul's desire was to serve God in every way he could, to put God's cause first, to put his own flesh under submission to the will of God. He knew that only by serving God first could he experience the fullness of life that Jesus promised every believer.

Jesus has our very best in mind at all times. The One who died for us is always working things out for our benefit, but we have to trust and serve Him first.

The Qualities of a Serving Heart

The Bible gives us a fascinating picture of a pair of women who exemplify a life of service. Martha and Mary were sisters who lived with their brother, Lazarus, in Bethany, and were dear friends of Jesus. When Jesus traveled through their area, He stayed at their home.

Martha had a servant's heart and great faith. These two characteristics go hand in hand. In fact, being a servant of Jesus takes great faith, because when we serve Him, we are not looking for immediate gratification; we believe that what we do will be rewarded by Him at a later time. We avoid acting out of present-day results for ourselves; we work to benefit someone else, just as a slave works for the benefit of his master.

This is what Luke writes about Martha's servant heart: "As Jesus and the disciples continued on their way to Jerusalem, they came to a village where a woman named Martha welcomed them into her home" (Luke 10:38). Have you met women like Martha? They look out for the welfare of others. She was determined that her Master would be welcome in her home and that she would provide for Him. She even began preparing a meal that was above the ordinary. Looking out for the welfare of others is one of the qualities of a serving faith. This means an active pursuit. It can come in many forms: providing hospitality, providing comfort, meeting needs, praying, speaking a kind word, and so forth.

I don't know why Luke mentions Martha in this verse, except perhaps to note that it was her hospitality from the first that welcomed Jesus into their home. But Martha is also like many women: We get caught up in the service and forget the more important goal. Luke writes:

> Her sister, Mary, sat at the Lord's feet, listening to what he taught. But Martha was worrying over the big dinner she was preparing. She came to Jesus and said, "Lord, doesn't it seem unfair to you that my sister just sits here while I do all the work? Tell her to come and help me."
> But the Lord said to her, "My dear Martha, you are so upset over all these details! There is really only one thing worth being concerned about. Mary has discovered it—and I won't take it away from her" (Luke 10:39-42).

How I can relate to Martha's complaints! Wasn't that exactly what I was doing early in my ministry when I let the housework, meal preparation and other details turn me into a sour hostess? I had lost sight of the goal—ministering in Jesus' name.

My major in college was Home Economics, so I love to see a well-set table sparkling with crystal and china and cut flowers, a meal with gourmet flavors and all the other fine touches that go along with entertaining guests. These are all appropriate in certain circumstances, but how easy it is to let these preparations become so overwhelming that they destroy the spirit of a serving faith.

Therefore, this is the second quality of a serving faith: A person keeps the goal of the service as the main focus. Mary understood that listening to Jesus was more important than eating a big meal. Martha should have whipped up a casserole, cut up some fresh vegetables, and thrown in a quick dessert! Then both she and Mary could have relaxed at the feet of Jesus while they waited for dinner to finish cooking.

John writes about another incident in Martha's life. You've probably heard the story of when Lazarus, her brother, died, was wrapped in burial clothing and put into a tomb. When Jesus arrived on the scene, Lazarus had been dead four days, and the sisters were heartbroken. While Mary stayed home, Martha went out to meet Jesus. When she saw Him outside the village, she said, "Lord, if you had been here, my brother would not have died. But even now I know that God will give you whatever you ask" (John 11:21).

Do you see Martha's faith in that statement? Her trust was in Jesus. She believed He could do anything. John continues with the story:

> Jesus told her, "Your brother will rise again."
>
> "Yes," Martha said, "when everyone else rises, on resurrection day."
>
> Jesus told her, "I am the resurrection and the life. Those who believe in me, even though they die like everyone else, will live again. They are given eternal life for believing in me and will never perish. Do you believe this, Martha?"
>
> "Yes, Lord," she told him. "I have always believed you are the Messiah, the Son of God, the one who has come into the world from God" (John 11:23-27).

After talking to her Lord, Martha went back to Bethany to get her sister, Mary. When the two women came to the grave, Jesus cried with them because He loved Lazarus so much. Then Jesus came to the cave and told the men to roll away the stone.

John writes, "Martha . . . said, 'Lord, by now the smell will be terrible because he has been dead for four days!'

"Jesus responded, 'Didn't I tell you that you will see God's glory if you believe?'" (John 11:39-40).

Jesus prayed to His Father in heaven and called for Lazarus to come out; and Martha's brother, still in his grave clothes, walked out of the tomb! Jesus had responded to Martha's faith, and she became witness to one of the greatest miracles of Jesus' ministry! What joy they all expressed as they unwrapped Lazarus's grave clothes!

This shows us another quality about serving faith: A person who has serving faith will see great and mighty things happen as a result of God's work in her life.

John records one more incident in the life of Mary and Martha. Later, right before the Passover was celebrated, Jesus once again came to their home. John writes, "A dinner was prepared in Jesus' honor. Martha served, and Lazarus sat at the table with him. Then Mary took a twelve-ounce jar of expensive perfume made from essence of nard, and she anointed Jesus' feet with it and wiped his feet with her hair. And the house was filled with fragrance" (John 12:2-3). Mary didn't realize it at the moment, but she was helping to prepare Jesus for His greatest trial and most astounding act, His death on the cross.

This is the final quality of serving faith that we will mention: A person with serving faith always gives praise to our Lord Jesus Christ. In the Bible, a sweet aroma symbolizes the praises we send heavenward. In Mary's home that day, the air was filled with fragrance. That was the desire of the sisters' servant hearts. Above all, they wanted to honor Jesus with their lives.

Joseph, that Old Testament saint, was an example of a man who had a deep and honest serving faith. He served his master, Potiphar, faithfully, and Potiphar's household thrived. One day, Potiphar's wife accused Joseph of making unwanted sexual advances toward her. Her accusations were completely false, yet Potiphar had Joseph thrown into jail on her testimony, and Joseph lost his good position and his reputation. In spite of it all, Joseph's attitude remained faithful to serving the Most High. He didn't let devastating circumstances come between him and his God.

As Joseph's faith illustrates, serving faith acts without expecting something in return. Martin Luther writes:

If you are called as a pastor or teacher, or if you are in some other position, set this goal for yourself: I will do my job faithfully without expecting any reward from the people I serve. I won't assume that they will be grateful to me. Rather, I will bless others the same way my heavenly father hands out his blessings. He gives money, talents, peace, and health to even the most ungrateful and evil people. I will remember Christ's command, "You must be perfect as your

Father in heaven is perfect" (Matthew 5:48). This means that we must serve people who are wicked, undeserving, and ungrateful. A few will acknowledge our service and thank us. But the others might even threaten our lives.

Sometimes we can get so caught up in our activities that we supplant our serving faith with mere busyness. For example, the lessons we prepare for teaching a children's Sunday School class become a burden because we don't allot enough time for preparation. The potluck dish we throw together is a bother because we didn't plan a trip to the grocery store. The commitment we made to help a neighbor turns into a hardship because our attitude deteriorates over time. Our serving faith turns into grudging service. Or we become so busy with our own activities that we push our service to others out of our schedule.

True serving faith asks two questions of each activity:

1. What can I do to help you?
2. Who gets the praise?

If we focus on these two priorities, we will be acting out of serving faith rather than other less-than-honorable attitudes. That's because serving faith focuses on others and gives the glory to God. Keep these questions in mind to help keep your priorities set in the right direction.

Servant Leadership

How many leadership positions do you hold? Before you answer, think of all the ways in which you influence people in your life. Each one of those areas is a place in which you serve as a leader. You don't have to be given a title such as CEO or manager to be a leader. In God's kingdom, a leader is grown up from spiritual roots to influence people around her.

Are you a wife or mother? That means you are a leader. Are you a Sunday School teacher, a nursery worker, the only believer in your office? Then you definitely are a leader. Do you have unsaved relatives or friends who have strayed from living their lives for the Lord? Then you are called upon to be a leader.

In the New Testament, leadership always means servanthood. We must always go back to the example of Jesus. He called Himself the Good Shepherd. What does a shepherd do? He leads his sheep. He doesn't whip them into shape or let them choose their own path. He goes before them to show them the safest way to travel. That's our role as a leader in God's kingdom.

Has a Visionary View

A servant leader has certain qualities. One is that she is a visionary. She can see beyond the circumstances or the program to God's perspective on the people she's serving. Doesn't that fit in well with our definition of faith—that we see what's in the future, what we hope for rather than merely what's in front of us?

Carl Combs, who is Director of International Leadership Academies for our ministry, tells a delightful true story about the importance of being a leader and setting sights on the visionary goal.

The event took place in the early 1900s in the manufacturing plant of the James H. Birch Carriage Company in Burlington, New Jersey. Birch's success with vehicle manufacturing attracted the attention of young, not yet well-known, Henry Ford. Ford was fascinated with Birch's use of assembly-line procedures. During a meeting, Ford approached Birch with an offer to partner in a new endeavor to build automobiles with an assembly-line approach, using Birch's plans.

Birch's company made some of the finest vehicles in the world and was seeing great success in the business world. He declined Ford's offer but did decide to use Ford's axle and hub assembly on his vehicle. So the two men hammered out an agreement for Birch to use the Ford parts. Birch continued to make his carriages and passed up an opportunity to build an assembly line for Ford's "tin lizzie." Combs explains what happened:

> The owner's son, Mr. James H. Birch, Jr., a progressive merchandiser, wanted to convert to automobiles. His father

took an adamant stand. The 1907 Birch catalogue carried a full-page picture showing a horse gaily trotting past two automobiles stranded in ditches. The caption read, "The Passing of the Horse."

Today, Mr. James H. Birch of Burlington, New Jersey, stands out in the memories of people who file through the Burlington Corson-Poley Center to view possibly the only remaining evidence of a well-managed company that lacked visionary, market-tracking leadership: a human-drawn rickshaw with Ford hubs!

Sounds silly to us now, doesn't it? A rickshaw trying to take the place of the new automobile that had just been invented! What a lack of vision Birch had! Sadly, many Christians get caught up in producing the same old programs, using tired methods, and then wonder why their ministry goes nowhere.

Here at Campus Crusade, we have always followed a certain pattern. Our message never changes. It is always the same gospel that Jesus gave us to spread throughout the world. But if you look at the ways in which the staff presents this message, you will find great innovation and creativity. Our goal is to meet the needs of the person to whom we are sent.

That's what vision is all about—seeing the needs of others and meeting them. A serving faith looks beyond what "we've always done" to "what God wants us to do now." That's how we keep our vision fresh and our leadership strong. This is also how we fit our leadership style into serving faith.

What are you involved in right now that applies to servant leadership? How can you look up from the entanglement of the present to see where you want to lead?

Leads by Example

Another element of servant leadership is leading by example. I was inspired by this story of humble leadership.

On Monday, December 22, 2003, at the Shiloh Baptist Church in Alexandria, Virginia, the streets were choked with police, roads

were blocked and Secret Service agents roamed the church hallways. At about 3:00 P.M., a car pulled up and President and Mrs.
George W. Bush stepped out. Along with them were hordes of re-
porters with their cameras.

President Bush and his wife entered the church building and
greeted 40 inner-city kids who had been assembled as part of the
Angel Tree, a Prison Fellowship ministry to prisoners' children. At
Christmas time, hundreds of thousands of volunteers deliver gifts
to more than 500,000 children of inmates. President and Mrs.
Bush were two of those volunteers.

The First Couple stayed to talk to the children and their mothers and grandmothers and to have photos taken with them. At the
same time, Al Lawrence, a member of the Prison Fellowship staff,
came up to the President to greet him. Al had once been a prisoner
but had found Jesus Christ, and his life had been transformed. The
President threw his arms around this African-American ex-prisoner
to greet him.

Surely, with all President and Laura Bush had to do, especially
around the holidays, 40 inner-city children's welfare may have easily been overlooked. The most powerful man in our nation took
time to care for those who were the most powerless in our society!
That's serving faith.

Thinks of Others First

Another element of servant leadership is that it leaves no room for
ego. Pride destroys what we attempt to do for our Lord. God warns
us in Proverbs 11:2, "Pride leads to disgrace, but with humility
comes wisdom." How many wonderful Christian ministries have
been damaged by the pride of its leader or those who minister to
others? Keep the goal in mind: think of others first. This will be a
deterrent for letting your ego run the show.

Teaches Others to Lead

A third element of servant leadership is giving people room to
grow. Paul showed us how to do this. His pattern of ministry was
to go into a new town, preach in the synagogue and other public

areas, and form a church. Then he trained the new believers before he left to go to a new place. He still kept in contact with the church he founded, giving them advice and encouragement, but he allowed these new believers to take on leadership roles and make decisions. He was a mentor rather than an authoritarian dictator.

As a parent, the temptation is to retain tight control so that your children will not experience the hardships you have encountered and the mistakes you may have made. But this will not allow your children to develop their own spiritual strength. The same principle applies to Christians in your area of ministry. You must allow them freedom to express their style of growth and leadership.

We have lived by this principle in our ministry. We believe that the Holy Spirit works in the lives of believers, and our responsibility is to just give training and allow the Spirit to control the direction and flow of the ministry. When a person receives Christ as Savior, they are trained and sent out to share their faith right away. We train our staff to train other believers to train other believers in a chain that develops many leaders rather than pooling the leadership within a few hands. This discipleship chain relies on the talents of many people rather than just a few.

Executes the Vision

Another element of servant leadership is not only to have a far-reaching, heavenly vision, but also to have good management skills. What is the difference between vision and management? Vision sets the direction in which to go. Management handles the details of getting there. Both are needed to achieve the goal.

You can see how this works in your own home. You have a goal for raising godly children. That's your vision. But how do you achieve this goal? That's where you employ your management skills. Perhaps one of your management techniques will be to maintain family devotions with your children each evening. Also, church and Sunday School attendance would be part of the management area. You can apply this principle to any of your spiritual goals.

I thank Bill for gently pushing me into leadership positions. He was always so supportive of what I felt God wanted me to do.

He shared generously of the opportunities of ministry and was a Christian example in living the servant leadership he professed. His confidence in me, his encouragement, his love, his protective concern and his availability, along with his determination that I be "my own person," provided inspiration and motivation as I sought to be God's maximum woman for each stage and opportunity in my life. Now I realize that Bill's confidence in me gave me confidence that I was capable of doing anything God called me to do.

We can accomplish this for each other, for those we serve, for the Body of Christ, as we serve in our leadership positions. God will honor our attitude of servant leadership as we continue to work under His direction and control.

Serving Faith Begins at Home

God has given women an immense task—to serve others at home. If you are a mother of more than one preschooler, or of a teenager, you are probably nodding your head right now, agreeing that your tasks are almost beyond your capabilities at times. Demands from a husband, children, household tasks, a job, ministry, civic responsibilities and so many other essential duties seem overwhelming. Yet this arena of serving faith is where we are most effective. What we do in our homes will have the most lasting consequences of anything else we do.

Every wife and mother is an entrepreneur. This implies creativity, innovation and the ability to see potential where others don't even see the opportunity. This is where the visionary aspect of your leadership comes in. You know where you want to go.

The technical part of the job is pulling together just the right ingredients to make the dream a reality. This is where the vision begins to take shape in practical objectives. This is when the managerial skills come in to play to put the ingredients into perspective and realize the sequence and timing to put the dream into a part of the big picture. These are the detailed steps that bring about accomplishment.

Here's an example of how this process of vision and management works out in real life. It's Monday morning, and your weekend was filled with family activities and church. When you come into the kitchen, you find the milk container sitting on the counter, and it's empty. Within moments, your children will be ready to devour a bowl of cereal with milk. What to do? The entrepreneurial part of you says, "I'll scramble eggs and make toast in the shape of stars!"

When the hungry children converge in the kitchen and discover a breakfast table with eggs and toast in the shape of stars, their eyes pop open wider. Then you announce, "This week, you're all going to be stars. Real stars. Let's thank God for the food and ask Him to help you shine brightly."

By mid-week, you find a few moments to glance at the calendar and define your priorities. Your son has a science project due, and you have not purchased the items he needs. In fact, you don't even have a list of what you need to buy. Your daughter has volunteered to bring cookies to her youth group meeting, and you don't remember the last time you smelled the aroma of chocolate chip cookies filling your kitchen. Now you need the technician part of your leadership abilities. You make a trip to the craft store for the science project items, and while you leave the store, your mind flashes to the sugar canister on the kitchen counter. It's empty. So you make a quick stop at the grocery store on your way home. By the end of the afternoon, before Mom's Taxi Service goes into service, you have baked the cookies and planned the science project.

By bedtime, your tired family retires for the night. The manager in you comes out, however, when you see the jumble of backpacks in the living room. You line them up by the back door, throw in a load of towels to wash, and check to see if you have milk for the morning.

Sometimes this may all seem overwhelming—and sometimes it is. But when you have an attitude of servant leadership, you are able to manage each part of your leadership role in a more effective and godly way. Servant leadership comes from an attitude of the heart, and you cannot do it in your own strength. It is only as you yield to the Holy Spirit's control that you can lead with joy. Your goal is not merely to make the family run smoothly, but to enable your children to grow and mature and fulfill their responsibilities. At times, this may mean stepping back and letting them take over responsibilities as they are able. Other times it may mean stretching yourself so that they can benefit from your leadership.

We are called upon to sacrifice for our families. That means keeping our husbands as a first priority in our lives, and our children as our second priority. (After God, of course.)

Bill's mother was an example of such a godly woman. She was known as a woman of prayer and as a woman of the Book. Her children could always count on her.

Bill's family lived in rural Oklahoma, and he took the bus home after school. In the winter, darkness would fall before the bus left him off down the country road.

One day, a blizzard had come up, and when Bill stepped off the bus after his day at elementary school had ended, the snow almost blinded him. He began stumbling his way up the country road, slipping into the ruts hidden by the snow. Snow filled his boots and stung his face.

Then he saw a light in the distance. It was getting brighter. He knew it was his mother, coming to meet him with a lantern. She had left the warmth of her house to help her son find his way home in the dark. Even though he had told her not to do this, she still felt she must. Tears slipped down his face as he saw her emerge from the darkness.

How many people give testimony to the fact that their godly mother influenced them to live for Jesus? Countless. How many husbands have said, like the man in Proverbs 31, "There are many virtuous and capable women in the world, but you surpass them all!" (Prov. 31:29)? Our servant leadership at home is vital. It is the greatest calling we have.

For those of you who are single, you have no less of a calling than women with husbands and children. Whenever I think of the influence of single women, instantly Dr. Henrietta Mears comes to mind. She is the one who led me to faith in Christ. I learned so much from her as she mentored me. For 10 years, Bill and I lived with her in the Bel Air mansion. I can't imagine what Campus Crusade for Christ would be like today without her influence. At one point in her life, a tall Dartmouth graduate asked for her hand in marriage. Dr. Mears yearned for a home and a family, yet after great inner conflict, she turned him down because he didn't share her faith in Christ. In time, God called her into full-time ministry. She was a woman of God!

In her lifetime, she established Gospel Light Publications, which transformed the way Sunday Schools were handled; Forest Home Conference Center, which is still being used by God to bring thousands to Christ; and Gospel Light Worldwide, which helps meet the literature needs of new churches and missions around the world. As a single woman, God has a unique and wonderful place for you also as a servant leader in His Body. But remember, you must rely upon the person of the Holy Spirit to control your attitude, your actions and ultimately the result of your actions.

When we fail in our duties, we only have to confess that we are depending upon our own strength—then we ask God's forgiveness and give Him control over our acts of leadership. We leave the results in His hands.

Serving Faith in Ministry

More than 8,000 orphans called her Mama—the offspring of Muslims, Christians and pagans. But to Lillian Trasher, they were only babies who desperately needed food, clothing, a place to sleep and, as much as anything else, a mother's love.

On October 8, 1910, Lillian and her sister Jennie sailed for Egypt with no support of a mission board and just enough money to make their way to the home of a missionary Lillian had met before she left home in America.

When the sisters arrived in Egypt, Lillian, the outgoing, more aggressive younger sister with a "can-do" personality, was ready to set Egypt on fire, but she wasn't exactly sure where the matches were. Her life ministry unfolded in one of those almost larger-than-life stories in which God uses an ordinary person to accomplish extraordinary feats when the odds are impossibly stacked against success.

Lillian had been in Egypt for barely three months when there was a loud, disconcerting knock at the door. It was evening, and no guests were expected. Lillian jumped to her feet as the door was opened. A man, half crying, spoke Arabic in staccato bursts as he explained that an Egyptian woman was dying, and he pleaded for someone to come help.

Lillian threw her coat around her shoulders as she said, "Let me go!" Reverend Dunning, the man who had invited the sisters to come work with him, was more than happy to stay behind as Lillian and two Egyptian coworkers followed the stranger.

Entering a smelly, windowless hut, their eyes slowly became accustomed to the darkness. Lying on a straw pallet was a young woman. Lillian knelt by her side. Suddenly the young mother, perhaps sixteen years of age, opened her eyes, looked into Lillian's face and cried out, "Arjouky, arjouky! Takhdihom!" Moments later she died.

Then Lillian noticed a newborn baby, a tiny undernourished infant, lying in the lap of an old woman. A weak cry came from the lips of the struggling infant who flailed its tiny arms. Lillian shrank back.

One of the Egyptian coworkers softly asked, "Mees Lillian, do you know what that young mother said to you before she died?" Then looking away, he said, "She wanted you to please take the baby home with you."

The old lady forcibly placed the tiny child in Lillian's arms, who, not knowing what to do, took the infant back to the missionary compound. Was this her mission in life? The circumstances all were against it. At the missionary compound, the cries of the tiny infant, badly undernourished and slowly dying, kept the rest of the missionaries awake nights. Finally the director told her, "Either you take the baby back to the village or you have to leave."

She left. With barely enough money to rent an empty house and only enough money for food that would last a week, the orphanage at Assiout, Egypt, on the banks of the Nile River, was begun.

Lillian had launched a lasting work with the orphanage, but it was not what she had planned. Her faith in God took her to a mission field and her availability allowed her to be mightily used by God.

Servant faith in ministry means: Please be available to God.

Women in the Bible played many different roles in life while still being faithful to their call as wives and mothers. Today, the way is clearly open for women to use their time outside the home in more ways than we have ever been able to do before. Women are liberated to choose what they wish to do; yet the woman seeking God's direction will find freedom by following the leading of the Holy Spirit in her life. For some, quitting their jobs or curtailing their activities away from home will be most honoring to Christ; however, for others, seeking employment or getting involved in volunteer activities is God's pathway for them. Because Christ is working in and through her, a Christian woman's ministry will be revolutionary.

God wants to give us our desires: "Take delight in the LORD, and he will give you your heart's desires. Commit everything you do to the LORD. Trust Him, and he will help you" (Ps. 37:4-5). In many circumstances, I have had to say, "Lord, if this desire isn't of You, take it away. If it is of You, keep it prominent in my thinking." When I'm assured that it's from God, then I prayerfully ask for direction for how my desire can be fulfilled. As I wait for my prayers to be answered, I find the answers in God's perfect timing—not always in my timetable, but in His perfect timing. God is faithful to fulfill all His promises.

Serving faith in ministry also means: Bear one another's burdens. Martin Luther writes, "Everywhere love turns it finds burdens to carry and ways to help. Love is the teaching of Christ. To love means to wish another person good from the heart. It means to seek what is best for the other person." Luther bases his words on Galatians 6:2: "Share each other's troubles and problems, and in this way obey the law of Christ."

Sharing another's burdens doesn't mean taking them over, but encouraging, comforting, coming alongside as they handle their own problems. This is a vital part of a servant faith.

Recently, I co-authored a series of novels with a delightful writer, Nancy Moser. In 'Round the Corner, you will meet a widow by the name of Evelyn Peerbaugh. When her husband dies suddenly, she is left without adequate income to support herself. To make up the difference, she opens her Victorian home as a boarding house.

One day, Evelyn finds herself visiting a friend in the hospital. As she makes her way down the hall, she unexpectedly volunteers to carry a vase of flowers to a patient, an elderly woman named Accosta Rand. Evelyn finds out that Accosta is going to be released from the hospital, but she has no family living near to help her get back home. Evelyn volunteers to be the one.

When Evelyn brings the frail woman home, she finds the refrigerator bare. She goes to the grocery store and buys enough food to last for a few days. When she arrives back at the home, she fixes chicken noodle soup and cleans up the house.

That's the spirit of serving faith—being available, seeing people's needs, acting on what God wants us to do out of love. This is living faith in action.

Closely related to serving faith is a giving faith. It, too, comes from a heart filled with God's love for others. In our next section, we will see how giving faith leads us into a life of high adventure and miracles.

A Pathway to Deepen My Faith

1. Learning from the Chapter
Are you currently serving God through a serving ministry? Look at the two areas mentioned in the chapter that refer to having a serving faith in ministry. Consider how you can make each aspect a clear part of your life and ministry.

Psalm 37:4-5: *Be available to God.* How can you make yourself more available to God where you serve?

_____

_____

_____

_____

_____

Galatians 6:2: *Bear one another's burdens.* How are you practicing this biblical mandate? What do you need to change
to be more effective?

_____

_____

_____

_____

_____

2. Knowing God's Word

The following verses teach us about serving God. Read each verse
and write down one way you can serve God.

Romans 6:6

_____

_____

_____

_____

_____

1 Chronicles 28:9

_____

_____

_____

_____

_____

_____

Matthew 6:24

_____
_____
_____
_____
_____
_____

3. Applying God's Word

Read Luke 10:38-42. After reading this passage, note what Jesus considers important in servanthood. Relate Martha's experience to how you handle your acts of service to others.

_____
_____
_____
_____
_____
_____

How much time are you spending at the feet of Jesus? To check yourself in this area, for one day, record how much time you spend reading your Bible and praying. Are you meditating on God's Word?

_____
_____
_____
_____
_____
_____

7

A Giving Faith

You can give without loving, but you cannot love without giving.
MAMIE McCULLOUGH

God has a giving nature, which He has built into His creation. Everything in this world is part of a give-and-take cycle. Without the process of giving back what has been endowed, life could not exist. For example, one element of our life essentials is the hydrologic cycle. That's the technical term for how water is recycled over and over for the benefit of all creation and so that life is refreshed with drinkable water.

We've all felt and smelled the sweetness of an afternoon rain shower. The clouds are releasing their heavy load of water. But where did this water come from?

That's part of the hydrologic cycle. The rain causes surface runoff where water runs along the surface of the land into bodies of water or soaks down into the soil to become groundwater. This makes fresh water available to plants and animals. In turn the bodies of water on earth—lakes, rivers, oceans—are sources of evaporation. When droplets of water warm, they rise into the atmosphere. Eventually, the water vapor in the atmosphere cools enough so that it condenses and forms new clouds. When these clouds get too heavy with water, once again it rains.

Nowhere in this cycle does a part of nature decide to stop the flow of water and hoard it. We can see this truth everywhere, and we depend on it for life.

God has created many more giving cycles in nature. In the cycle of plants, a tree produces fruit, which drops off the tree onto the ground and decays, allowing the new seed to be fertilized and grow to produce more fruit.

One cycle in the forest seems like the opposite of giving on the surface, but actually assures the replenishing of the forest. Each summer, oak trees produce acorns, which fall to the ground. Squirrels pick them up and bury them and store them for the long winter months. It would seem as if the squirrels were interrupting the cycle of giving. But amazingly, they are part of the renewal. The squirrel's hoarding practices help the trees. During lean years, all the acorns will be eaten. But in plentiful years, the squirrels will leave many nuts behind. These buried seeds sprout and grow into new oaks. These new oaks eventually produce new crops of nuts for the squirrels. Each element in nature gives up its share so that all nature benefits.

The principle of giving was an essential part of the Early Church. The new believers understood God's giving nature. Many of the people who comprised the body of believers soon after Christ's resurrection had very few worldly goods. Because of the persecution they endured, some had almost nothing, yet they still gave. Paul commends the giving actions of the churches in Macedonia:

> Now I want to tell you, dear friends, what God in his kindness has done for the churches in Macedonia. Though they have been going through much trouble and hard times, their wonderful joy and deep poverty have overflowed in rich generosity. For I can testify that they gave not only what they could afford but far more. And they did it of their own free will. They begged us again and again for the gracious privilege of sharing in the gift for the Christians in Jerusalem. Best of all, they went beyond our highest hopes, for their first action was to dedicate themselves to the Lord and to us for whatever directions God might give them (2 Cor. 8:1-5).

What giving faith they had! They didn't consider themselves limited by what they had, but they just opened themselves up to any direction the Lord might lead them. No wonder Paul was so proud of their attitude!

A fascinating example of giving faith and its rewards is found in Acts 9. Dorcas was a woman who was noted for her giving spirit. She helped the poor, making clothing for those who had little to wear. When she died, her home was filled with mourners who came to show everyone what she had made for them. In their sorrow, her friends sent for Peter.

When Peter arrived, he shooed everyone out of the room where Dorcas's body lay. Then, through the power of prayer and the Holy Spirit, Peter raised Dorcas back to life. The news of the miracle flew all over town, and many more people believed in Jesus! Dorcas's reputation for giving faith had produced a multitude of spiritual fruit.

The people of the Early Church were concerned about each other. Luke writes, "All the believers were of one heart and mind, and they felt that what they owned was not their own; they shared everything they had" (Acts 4:32). Can you imagine what it must have been like to have enjoyed their fellowship? Would their giving faith have made you excited or would it have revealed your lack of giving?

In our society, we own so much more than those people did. America is by far the richest country in the world. We have more cars, more computers, more beautiful homes than any other place in the world. Why then, since we have so much, do we have so many locks? Just think of how our cars have changed over the years. When cars were first available on the market, they didn't even have keys! No one locked a car door. Then keyed ignitions were added, but you could take the keys out and leave the car in an unlocked position. The car could be started without a key in the ignition.

Today, we have car alarms, kill switches and LoJacks to keep our cars safe. It's not because cars are so rare and hard to obtain. Every family has at least one car. But our social attitude has changed. Our society has become more materialistic and less concerned for the other person. It's all centered around what I want!

We cannot throw away our keys and open up our homes to everyone; that would invite disaster. But we can learn how to have a giving faith that reflects our Father's heart. We can make an impact on our corner of the world like Dorcas did on hers. We can be wise and generous at the same time.

Our giving faith comes directly from God. He is the greatest giver. Of course, the greatest gift He gave was His Son, Jesus Christ. What are some of the characteristics of that gift?

He gave before He saw any response. Second Timothy 1:9 says, "It is God who saved us and chose us to live a holy life. He did this not because we deserved it, but because that was his plan long before the world began—to show his love and kindness to us through Christ Jesus." Even before we acknowledged who God is, He was calling us into His family. The verse also tells us that God gave to people who didn't deserve His gift. Certainly, none of us earned the gift of His love and forgiveness.

God's motivation was love. John 3:16 says, "For God so loved the world that he gave his only Son, so that everyone who believes in him will not perish but have eternal life." This verse expresses God's heart of love toward you and me. It also shows that God gave to everyone—not just to the rich or good-looking or talented. Every person ever born was worthy of God's gift.

God gives generously. "Tell those who are rich in this world not to be proud and not to trust in their money, which will soon be gone. But their trust should be in the living God, who richly gives us all we need for our enjoyment" (1 Tim. 6:17). God doesn't hold back anything that is for our good. He also gives us all we need to accomplish His purposes.

Jesus provided the example of a lifestyle of giving faith. Have you ever considered these facts?

- Jesus never had a savings account.
- He didn't buy a house—big or small.
- He didn't wear expensive clothing.
- He didn't waste His time on frivolous activities. (That doesn't mean He didn't take time to enjoy His friends.)
- He didn't eat in the fanciest restaurants.
- He didn't try to gain the favor of powerful people so that He could work His way up the ladder of success.

What did Jesus do? He healed the sick, even spending time with those pariahs of society of His day, the lepers. He took time out for children. He spent His day teaching people about God's kingdom. He was friends with everyone—the rich, the poor, the sinners, the religious elite. His main focus was not in building an empire on earth, but in furthering God's kingdom in heaven.

In fact, Jesus spoke more about giving than about almost any other subject He taught. Half of His recorded parables concern stewardship of money, property, time, talents and material possessions. Luke 6:38 gives His principle of giving: "If you give, you will receive. Your gift will return to you in full measure, pressed down, shaken together to make room for more, and running over. Whatever measure you use in giving—large or small—it will be used to measure what is given back to you."

Once again, we see that God considers giving a cycle of action. Jesus teaches that whatever you give, you will receive back at some time. Whether your reward will be today, tomorrow or in heaven, the cycle will not be broken.

Giving by Faith

If we receive rewards from God for our giving, then why do we need faith to give? Because our giving needs to spring from our life of faith, not from our own efforts to do good deeds. Let's face it: The majority of us are not naturally generous. Our inward nature is selfish.

Have you ever had thoughts like these?

I want to keep this for me!
This is mine and no one else can have it!
If I give this away, what will be left for me?
I'm afraid to give this up because next week I may need it.
No one's going to help me if I need something, so I'll just
keep what I have.

We must not be content to live under our old selfish nature. Our response must be this: Since God has given me so much, how can I hold back anything from Him? I will follow His example of abundantly sharing what I have.

Philippians 4:19 describes giving by faith in a nutshell: "This same God who takes care of me will supply all your needs from his glorious riches, which have been given to us in Christ Jesus."

The first step in giving by faith is to realize that God takes care of us. No matter how wealthy we are, without God, everything we have could be gone tomorrow. On the other hand, no matter how poor we are, we will never lack anything we need, because God is taking care of us. So we can put aside all our worries and trust God.

Step two is to realize that God will supply for our giving by faith. People and things all have their limitations. When I see the sad stories of the formerly rich CEOs who are now headed to prison for fraud, I understand the truth of this limitation. Howard Hughes died a wealthy man, but insane. His trust in his wealth did him no good. But we can always trust God to give us not whatever we want but what is best for us.

Step three is knowing that God supplies us out of His incredible riches. Our heavenly Father holds the treasures of heaven and earth in His hands. In good times and bad, His reserves remain stable and inexhaustible.

And step four is that our security is in God's riches given to us in Christ Jesus. Second Corinthians 8:9 says, "You know how full of love and kindness our Lord Jesus Christ was. Though he was very rich, yet for your sakes he became poor, so that by his poverty he could make you rich." If Jesus did that much for us, then we can surely place our faith in Him to supply everything we need. God bestows incredible gifts upon us because of Jesus. "How we praise God, the Father of our Lord Jesus Christ, who has blessed us with every spiritual blessing in the heavenly realms because we belong to Christ" (Eph. 1:3).

Ways to Give

Knowing what God, through Jesus, has given us, we must have a sense of urgency about our giving faith. How can we sit back and do nothing when our Father has lavished so much on us? We want to be like Jesus and spend our lives giving in faith as God leads us to give.

Give of Yourself

What comes to your mind when you think of giving faith? We frequently measure giving in dollars and cents, and yet the greatest sacrifice is in giving everything we are to God. Stewardship of ourselves requires purity in all we do and think. God created us for His glory. He wants to use us to further His kingdom and help us grow in faith.

Harriet Smith gave of herself. At her first training conference for staff of Campus Crusade, she heard about the need for a bilingual person with a heart for reaching Hispanics. After working with Hispanics in the United States and in Mexico for 14 years, she began ministering to the Chinese. She tells about her "switch" from one people group to another:

> I was translating a Missions Class for Dr. Roy Rosedale in Mexico City when he quoted a statistic that totally blew my mind: He said, "Ninety-seven percent of today's Christian workers are working in areas that are culturally close to Christianity, but only 5 percent of Christian workers are reaching out to the rest—more than half—of the world's population."

She had trouble even translating this statistic, not because she couldn't say it, but because of the impact it had on her life. She thought, *Who is going to tell the rest of the world?*

Leaving Mexico briefly to renew her visa, she found herself in a prayer meeting in Atlanta, where the focus was on prayer for unreached people groups, especially those of East Asia. At the end of the evening, she thought, *How could anyone be here tonight and not just want to pack her bags and go on the next plane to Asia?* She began praying about moving in that direction, but it took four years before she arrived at her Asian assignment. Harriet's ministry grew to be so successful—with so many people meeting Christ—that she had to leave, because too many people (and people in power) knew her main reason for being in China.

Returning to the U.S. and still having God's heart for the unreached people of East Asia, she began working with another Campus Crusade ministry that reaches out with the gospel to students from Mainland China while they are in the U.S. While her main role is in the office, she prefers opportunities to work directly with Chinese students. She networks with students, helping them connect with people who can continue the process of evangelism and discipleship as they move from one location to another. Harriet's influence for the Kingdom has been, and continues to be, invaluable!

I want to be very practical in how I define the giving of yourself. We have many different aspects to our personality and character; therefore you may have given part of yourself to God but withheld other parts.

Think about your tongue. Do you ever say something that you wish you had not said? Every word you speak will either uplift or tear down. If you are surrendered to Christ, the Holy Spirit will be a guard over your tongue, and you can control what you say. The next time you are tempted to respond harshly, take a deep breath, ask the Holy Spirit to help you, and experience the joy of knowing that you were giving the gift of restraint.

How about your thought life? Is it consecrated to the Lord or do you let it wander into areas that you know won't please Him? Are you listening to music that dishonors God? Watching movies or videos that portray scenes that you know are not moral? Give the gift of moral purity to God.

You can use every part of yourself to honor God. You are capable of doing acts of giving that reflect your unique abilities. He does not expect you to be like anyone else. God wants you to reflect His nature and glorify Him through who you are.

Give of Your Family
For most of us, our families, especially our children, are most precious. Most of our day is taken up in doing things for them. But

have you given them over to God? Or are you hoarding them for yourself?

In Campus Crusade's years of service, I have seen many wonderful young people whose hearts were torn by parents who couldn't give them up. This was a deep dilemma for these men and women. They felt a call from God to serve somewhere in the world, winning people to Christ, helping spread the gospel of Jesus Christ. Yet at the same time, their parents opposed their call because they didn't want to be separated from their children. This put these young men and women in such a difficult position.

We can hinder our children's lives in so many ways by not giving them up to God. This could be something as simple as talking them into participating in sports at school rather than in an outreach program with your church's youth group. This could mean filling our children's lives with so much activity from morning to night that they don't have time to spend reading their Bible or praying.

We, of course, should never neglect meeting the needs of our children and seeing to the needs of our aging parents as well. But when God asks us to let go, we must do what He says.

What would you do if your daughter announced that she had decided to move to one of the most dangerous places on earth to witness for Christ? What would you say if your son quit his lucrative job and moved his family, including your grandchildren, across the country to fill the pastorate in a small, rural church? If your children are still at home, do you allot plenty of time to encourage their spiritual growth, talk about important issues with them, get to know their friends and their activities?

An old African parable tells how monkey hunters in the jungle use special jars with long necks to trap their prey. They fill the jars with fruit and nuts and hang them from tree branches. As a monkey swings by, he spies the odd-looking objects in the tree and stops to investigate. Discovering that the jar is filled with food, he reaches in and grabs all he can hold in his hand.

With his fist clenched, however, he can't remove his hand through the narrow neck of the jar. No matter how he turns his bulging hand, it won't slide up through the neck. The solution is simple. All he has to do is let go of the fruit and nuts, and he can escape. But he doesn't. He holds on to his prize until the monkey hunter returns and grabs him.

We laugh at the foolishness and greediness of the monkeys risking their lives for a bit of food. But when we hold on selfishly to our families, not giving God total control over their lives, we act in a similar way. We lose the blessing that God has intended for us and for our loved ones.

Give of Your Talents

Mary Graham is a woman who consistently uses her talents for the Lord. She currently is associate Crusade staff and the president of Women of Faith, a weekend conference ministry designed to encourage women spiritually (presently drawing 10,000 to 20,000 women regularly). She joined our staff in 1969 after being personally challenged by Bill and me at a college reception. She told us, "The surprises that awaited me included developing my own financial support, taking all the initiative on the campus in evangelism, and being in over my head for the next 25 years."

Mary's time on staff has included working on a campus, being a traveling women's representative, working on the national U.S. team, and being the director of Women Today. Following a meeting with Luci Swindoll, who explained how God was using a new nationwide conference "Women of Faith," she was encouraged to see how Campus Crusade could help with the tremendous response to the conference. She became directly involved in this conference ministry, planning how to do follow-up with the women (sometimes more than 1,000!) who said they had received Christ at the conference. Her involvement in the conference continued to grow until Bill and I actually encouraged her to leave staff. God was working, and we realized that He had opened this particular door for Mary. It didn't make any difference that Campus Crusade's name wasn't on this ministry.

Once again, Mary wasn't certain what she was getting into, but she had the confidence to believe God and take her eyes off herself.

Another person who has given so much in service to our Lord is André Kole. He was one of the first people to join our staff and set up a specialized ministry within Campus Crusade. He had an idea: An illusionist could win thousands of people to Christ.

Bill and I had never thought of such an unusual strategy. Would it work? We didn't know of anyone who was performing magic in the name of Jesus Christ. But his enthusiasm was contagious. So we agreed to support his efforts.

Today, André Kole is still winning people to Christ through illusions. He has worked with various sizes of groups, including in huge auditoriums.

Recently, he performed in a 120-year-old church in Worcester, Massachusetts. As part of his act, he levitated over the stage in front of the massive organ pipes.

One-third of the people in the stone sanctuary were from the neighborhood, making André Kole's presentation the biggest evangelistic outreach in the church's history. After the gospel presentation, many indicated that they had invited Jesus into their lives.

What talents do you have? You may feel like you don't have much to contribute, but you would be wrong! You may be terrified to stand before people and speak. You may not feel that you have leadership skills. But your life speaks loudly of your level of faith, and you can pass on this faith and hope to others. A giving faith is one that can face the ordinary demands of a day and rise to the occasion with calm confidence that God will guide in every circumstance because He gives the abilities and power to accomplish all that He asks of us. You can be assured that He will never ask more than He has enabled you to fulfill, but that He will also stretch your giving faith as you give Him your talents and abilities to reach new heights of spiritual purpose!

Give of Your Time

Many years ago, during one of my mother's visits, we were invited to a luncheon at a friend's home. Mother was to be the honored guest, so we hurried madly to be on time. On the way, I realized that I had forgotten a folder of material I needed that afternoon, but we didn't have time to go back.

After lunch, I dashed to the beauty shop. As I sat under the hair dryer, images of the work in the folder that I should have been doing spoiled my concentration on the articles I was trying to read.

Leaving the shop slightly disgruntled, I planned to do my grocery shopping. As I walked in the supermarket door, it occurred to me that I had used my last check at the beauty shop and was out of cash. I resigned myself to the inconvenience and loss of time and decided to get the car washing done since I couldn't buy groceries. As I started to pay for the full tank of gas and car wash, I discovered I didn't have my credit card. (This was during the days when we filled our tanks first and paid last.) The woman helping me was very gracious and suggested I use an old ticket with my credit card number on it; however, the adjustment she had to make took a great deal of time and inconvenienced both of us. On my way home I rebuked myself quite sternly: *Oh, if you'd just taken a few moments to think through this afternoon . . . If you'd just picked up your folder, everything would have been so much better.* Engrossed in my unwise use of time, I absent-mindedly took a wrong turn on the freeway, which delayed my arrival home and inconvenienced me even further.

That was just one hectic afternoon in my life, but such events can permeate a person's entire lifetime. If you could talk with some of the women who have assisted me over the years, you would probably hear a recurring theme. "Mrs. Bright is just too available." Yes, that has been a source of frustration for many. Our home and our offices have been open, and we have attempted to respond to those who need us. This flexibility was necessary. Yet at the same time, I've learned that it is impossible to give of your time and energy without structure. To be truly free to give of yourself, you must manage your time well.

Basically, time management is thinking ahead and planning what you are going to do before you do it. It encompasses stewardship of your time, talent and treasure—of all that God has given you. Time management involves determining what you really want to accomplish and then putting those goals into your plans for a week, a year and a lifetime. Time management gives direction and balance. It helps you see the importance of what you are doing day to day, because your activities are bringing you closer to achieving your long-term goals.

Many times women feel that a schedule is limiting. They don't want to be organized because they like to do what they want, when they want. Of course, some consider this as liberating. However, I have found that nothing has liberated me more than when I have planned ahead, claiming God's wisdom. If we don't plan ahead, when we come to the end of life, having done "what comes naturally," we must be prepared to accept the fact that our lives may have counted for very little that is worthwhile. We may fulfill the old adage: If you aim at nothing, you will hit it.

It is important to remember, too, that time management is not designed to confine but to give the freedom to organize yourself to accomplish the things that you feel are important, worthwhile and contribute to making you the person you want to be.

Of course, when there are many, many, interruptions in a person's life, such as meeting the needs of small children, then you have to plan loosely. Then it is necessary to be less structured. However, it is especially important under these circumstances to know how you want to use your free time when you get it.

The parable of the talents as recorded in Matthew 25 is a significant illustration of managing yourself. Too frequently we think of giving only in the realm of our money. Giving of our resources is important, but more important than money is "you." Giving Christ all of you, totally surrendered to His purpose and plan for your life. The act of giving one's self to Christ may not seem so difficult; however, living out a surrendered life, moment by moment, is a different story. Let's look at a familiar parable and draw some conclusions.

The story concerns a master who, while planning a journey, entrusts a portion of his money to three servants. To one man he gives five talents, to another two and to another one talent, each according to his ability. Two of the men invest their money, but one man hides it so that he won't lose it. Upon his return, the master rewards the first and second servant because they have wisely handled the money they received and returned a profit to him. However, the master punishes the third servant because he hid his money and did not receive any profit from it. The story teaches us that if we don't use our time or what God has given us to the very best advantage, we find even that which has been given to us is taken away.

It's easy for us to make judgments about that third servant, but I would like to encourage you to take a look at your own life. Women have so many options today. We can choose to have a career and family and still find time to socialize. There is nothing wrong with being busy, but it is not good to allow busyness to rob us of opportunities to give of ourselves. Remember the three areas we have to give: time, talent and resources.

Take a quick assessment of your lifestyle. How do you spend the major portion of your hours each day? At the end of a week, if you made a list of how you "gave" of yourself, how many items are on your list? Unfortunately for many women, the giving part of life doesn't move beyond practical expectations. We become so overwhelmed with maintaining life that we have little time to respond to the needs of others.

Jesus modeled a wonderful example of what it means to move through life fulfilling the responsibilities of each day and yet always finding time to stop and meet the needs of people. I suggest that you study how He used His time by reading the Gospels: Matthew, Mark, Luke and John. Take notes about the ways He gave of Himself, then apply the principles of His giving to your daily schedule.

Give of Your Finances

In July 1903, a young man moved to Chicago to make his fortune. Although he had only a few years experience working with dairy products, he decided to set his theories about cheese making into operation. With only $65 in his pocket, a cart and a rented horse named Paddy, he began selling cheese to Chicago retail merchants. By the end of the first year, he owed $3,000. No one would give him more credit to buy more cheese, so he had to run his business on a cash-only basis day by day. His future didn't look good to most people.

He kept working hard, but he still wasn't making any money. One day, he decided to set a goal of selling $100 worth of cheese. He loaded his wagon and set off. But at the end of the day, he had only taken in $12.65. As he turned Paddy toward home, he felt beaten.

"Paddy, what's the matter with us anyhow?" he asked the horse.

Although Paddy couldn't talk, the young man felt like he received an answer. "You're working without God!" Right there, the young man decided to make God his partner.

Do you know who that man was? J. L. Kraft, founder of the Kraft Cheese company. The Lord blessed his commitment, and within a few years, he owned 50 subsidiaries with operations in Canada, Australia, England and Germany. When Bill met Mr. Kraft at a business meeting in the 1940s, in Hollywood, Bill was impressed with his godliness. Mr. Kraft was known to have donated up to one-third of his income to the cause of Christ.

If we put God first in our life, this will be reflected in our giving patterns. What we do with our money says so much about what our priorities are and what we treasure in our hearts. If a friend examined your checkbook, what would she see? Would she notice your giving faith or your spending habits? We all have financial responsibilities, but what do we do with the extra? Do we give a little here and there to the Lord, or do we have a definite plan for tithing (giving God at least 10 percent) and for special offerings where they are needed? Is our hand out when someone we love is in need? Or do we have clenched fists, keeping most of what we have for ourselves? Most of all, are we letting God guide the allocation of our paycheck, savings accounts, inheritance or any other assets we may have?

The old story is still true. When a man asked at a rich man's funeral, "How much did he leave when he died?" the answer was, "All of it."

Bill was such an example to me of giving faith. Even on the day we wrote our contract with the Lord where we listed what we wanted in the future, he was not concerned with material possessions but with giving his all to Jesus. He never owned a home, and we drove cars loaned to us from other people. Bill's interest in material possessions was in funneling whatever he could to fulfill the Great Commission in our lifetime.

One day he came to me with a great idea. It was a faith moment for him. It happened one night while he was listening to a sermon by Dr. Charles Stanley, pastor of the First Baptist Church in Atlanta, Georgia. Dr. Stanley was speaking on the blessings of giving by faith. What Bill felt impressed to do was give his pension fund to the ministry of Campus Crusade for the spreading of the gospel. He had turned 65 and could now give his pension as a lump sum for that purpose. He was so excited about being able to give a sum of that amount.

But where would he give it? He knew just where. Many years ago, before we were married, Bill had heard Dr. Oswald Smith challenge about a thousand college students and young singles to commit their lives to helping fulfill the Great Commission. He asked each person to place his or her name on a country and claim it for the Lord through prayer and finances. Bill had put his name on the Soviet Union.

Two years later, after we married, I joined him in praying for the Soviet Union. In 1978, we had the privilege of touring and speaking throughout the country. This was before the Iron Curtain fell in Eastern Europe and was open to the gospel. We accepted eagerly, and Bill spoke 18 times in eight cities to an audience of millions.

Of course, then the Iron Curtain fell, and the opportunities for ministry within Russia opened up all over the country. Now Bill had a chance to really impact the spread of the gospel in that great country! So that's what he did; he gave his pension to help spread the gospel in Russia. And he never regretted it for one moment!

Each of us must make our financial decisions in a unique way. We give our money to the Lord because it belongs to Him anyway, and He supplies us with what we need in the future. He blesses us with His marvelous grace and riches. And the cycle of giving faith is repeated over and over.

Give of Your Possessions

What do you own that is dear to you? Your home? A car? A treasured collection? Antique dishes or furniture?

You would be surprised what people treasure. In the newspaper one day, a story told of a couple who was getting a divorce. They had a collection of Beanie Baby stuffed toys. Both the husband and the wife wanted all of them, so they couldn't finalize their divorce because they were still fighting over who got the entire collection.

The judge in the case settled it by splitting the collection in half and giving half to each of the spouses. Of course, that decision made neither of them happy.

We think, *How ridiculous to be fighting over toys!* Yet we all have that tendency to hold on to our possessions. I'm sure you've felt that clutch inside your heart when you were expected to give up something you suddenly felt possessive about.

Sometimes, we can watch people act crazy over the smallest items. Have you ever been to an Easter egg hunt in a mall? All the parents and their little children line up to hunt for the eggs. The looks on the parents' faces tell it all. Many have gotten caught up in the moment of greed and aren't interested in seeing their child have a good time but are intent on getting all they can. And if a few of the eggs happen to hold dollar bills, the emotions intensify.

If you think about the situation logically, how valuable are those pieces of candy and a couple of dollar bills? Not very. But grabbing possessions is a powerful emotion that captures all of us at one time or another.

But if we give God ownership of all we have, we reflect His giving nature. And we are incredibly blessed.

Remember the contract Bill and I signed with God? Before signing that contract we each had made lists of our goals and desires. My desires were quite practical. I wanted to have two family cars and a comfortable home. The most important item on both our lists was the sincere desire to please God and be used by Him in all we did.

Looking back, I realize how wonderfully God has blessed our commitment to not allow material things to own us but to recognize that we can use every material blessing for His glory. Bill and I enjoyed driving fine vehicles and lived in a lovely home with Miss Mears prior to moving to Arrowhead Springs. We resolved to be happy with what God provided. We enjoyed much but we owned little. I am not telling you about our life's choices to imply that you should do likewise. I am illustrating the reality of what God can and will do when you are willing to trust Him for everything.

For a time, we lived in Bel Air, one of the most exclusive areas of Los Angeles. Then we moved to Arrowhead Springs, California, when it became Campus Crusade's international headquarters. Arrowhead Springs had formerly been the playground of the Hollywood stars! As part of the ministry, Bill and I saw millions and millions of dollars come into the ministry to be used for God's glory.

All this happened because we had turned our possessions over to God. I found out how rich God really is. That doesn't mean that every believer will see riches rain down. God has a unique plan for each of us. You may never see what God has in store for you until you meet Jesus in heaven.

I think of those saints of faith mentioned in Hebrews 11. They gave their all—their lives—for the cause of Christ. Yet they did not see any reward in this life. Instead, in human terms, their lives seemed to be full of tragedy and sorrow. But read what the book of Hebrews says about them:

Others trusted God and were tortured, preferring to die rather than turn from God and be free. They placed their hope in the resurrection to a better life. Some were mocked, and their backs were cut open with whips. Others were chained in dungeons. Some died by stoning, and some were sawed in half; others were killed with the sword. Some went about in skins of sheep and goats, hungry and oppressed and mistreated. They were too good for this world. They wandered over deserts and mountains, hiding in caves and holes in the ground.

All of these people we have mentioned received God's approval because of their faith, yet none of them received all that God had promised. For God had far better things in mind for us that would also benefit them, for they can't receive the prize at the end of the race until we finish the race (Heb. 11:35-40).

Giving faith is like that. It gives like God gives—without looking for something in return. It gives all—our best and our most treasured. It gives joyfully, with eyes toward the receiver of the gift rather than what the giving will do for us. And giving faith comes from the wealth of God's riches as He gives them to us to channel on to others. More important, those who give in faith are sure of their reward—in heaven, not necessarily here on earth.

How is your giving faith? Do you thrill with excitement over what God has given you so that you can give to others? Is your purpose to give so that God's kingdom will be magnified? Our giving faith is closely related to another facet of our faith—sharing faith. Through this act of service to others, we can give away our most precious gift, our faith in Christ.

A Pathway to Deepen My Faith

1. Learning from the Chapter
The chapter asked three important questions. Answer each one by giving specific details.

How active is your giving faith? What are the signs that you have a giving faith?

_____

_____

_____

_____

_____

Do you thrill with excitement over what God has given you so that you can give to others, or does your hand fall back when it is time to give?

_____
_____
_____
_____
_____
_____

Is your purpose to give so that God's kingdom will be magnified, or are you giving to gain your own credit?

_____
_____
_____
_____
_____
_____

2. Knowing God's Word
What does Philippians 4:19 say about the source of your giving?

_____
_____
_____
_____
_____
_____

Read the "hall of faith" chapter in Hebrews 11, and then write down any attitudes you see commended in the passage.

_____
_____
_____
_____
_____
_____

In your own words, write the principle of giving as stated in the following verse: Luke 6:38.

_____

_____

_____

_____

_____

_____

3. Applying God's Word
The four steps to giving are:

1. Realize that God takes care of you.
2. Recognize that God will supply everything you need for your giving by faith.
3. Affirm that God will supply your needs out of His incredible riches.
4. Place your security in God's riches, which are given to us in Christ Jesus.

Take these four steps, using them as you expand your giving by faith.

Below are listed the six ways we can give. After each, write what you are doing in this area of giving. When you see which area is lacking, consider how you can give more in that area of life. More than one may be part of the same ministry in which you are involved.

Give of Yourself

_____

_____

_____

_____

_____

_____

Give of Your Family

_____

_____

_____

_____

_____

_____

Give of Your Talents

_____

_____

_____

_____

_____

Give of Your Time

_____

_____

_____

_____

_____

_____

Give of Your Finances

_____

_____

_____

_____

_____

Give of Your Possessions

_____

_____

_____

_____

_____

Vonette's graduation from Texas Women's University (1948).

Young Vonette in 1954.

Vonette at home in Orlando, Florida (2010).

Vonette is honored with the Board of Directors Award at the National Religious Broadcasters Convention (2006).

Bill and Vonette Bright are married in Coweta, Oklahoma, on December 30, 1948.

Bill and Vonette attend a Navigator Conference at Star Ranch in Colorado (1952).

Vonette and Bill at Campus Crusade World Headquarters in Arrowhead Springs, California (1988).

The home that Bill and Vonette shared with Henrietta Mears from 1953-1963, 110 Stone Canyon Road, Bel Air, California.

Henrietta Mears in the drawing room of the Stone Canyon Home.

A social gathering in the drawing room of Miss Mears's home.

Vonette speaking to staff women at the Greig home in Mound, Minnesota (1958).

Vonette speaking to a women's group in her home at Arrowhead Springs, California.

Brad, Vonette and Zac in the garden at the Mears residence (Easter 1962).

Brad, Vonette and Zac in the conference center chapel in Mound, Minnesota (1961).

Brad, Vonette and Zac in the courtyard at Arrowhead Springs, Bungalow 10.

Vonette launches the Great Commission Prayer Crusade (1976).

Vonette in the prayer chapel at Arrowhead Springs, California.

Vonette was present when President Reagan signed the legislation establishing The National Day of Prayer.

Vonette speaking in Korea.

Bill, Vonette, Dale Evans and Roy Rogers on the set for the movie *Revolution Now* (1975).

Bill, Brad, Vonette and Zac prepare for a family vacation (1968).

Zac, Bill, Vonette and Brad in the courtyard at Bungalow 10, Arrowhead Springs, California.

Vonette and Brad in Breckenridge, Colorado.

Vonette is honored as a distinguished alum from Texas Women's University.

Vonette in the Soviet Union (1990).

Vonette and Bill in the Soviet Union (1991).

Vonette and Bill on a garden walk (1998).

Portrait of Vonette and Bill (1999).

Vonette, Bill and Steve Douglass taping the World Changers radio program (1995).

Vonette records the *Women Today* radio program (1994).

Zac, Bill, Vonette and Brad at Arrowhead Springs, California (Christmas 1974).

Bill could always make Vonette laugh, even during an interview.

Vonette and Bill at Lake Hart in Florida (1991).

The Brights celebrate their 50th wedding anniversay in Orlando, Florida.

Family photo of Vonette, Zac, Bill and Brad.

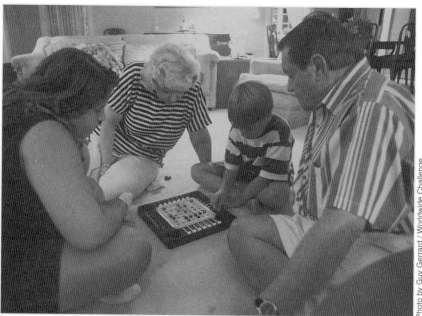

Vonette and Bill playing games with their grandchildren.

Photo by Guy Gerrard / Worldwide Challenge.

Vonette at the Global Pastors Network conference held at the Campus Crusade for Christ Headquarters (2003).

Vonette enjoys an elephant ride with a Campus Crusade staff director in Chang Mai, Thailand (March 2004).

Vonette's first photo taken after Bill's passing.

Photo by Guy Gerrard / Worldwide Challenge.

Portrait of Bill taken in 1994.

Photo by Guy Gerrard / Worldwide Challenge.

Vonette embraces her favorite photo of Bill (2004).

Photo by Guy Gerrard / Worldwide Challenge.

8

A Sharing Faith

*As we share with gentleness what has happened along our own
faith journey, we find that our dialogue conveys the message
that Jesus meant for us to carry.*

CHRISTOPHER COPPERNOLL

About a dozen ladies had gathered for an English tea in the garden
of one of their homes. The women were all anticipating a relaxing
time of conversation around some delightful cups of tea and
homemade scones. The azaleas were in bloom and the grass was
spring green. There's just something so wonderful about a meeting of women!

The conversation had barely begun and the scones were being
passed around the circle of friends when one of the younger women
gasped in delight. "Melissa, what's that on your finger?"

Everyone's head turned as Melissa proudly laid her slim hand
on the glass-topped patio table for everyone to see. A diamond engagement ring sparkled in the sunlight.

Immediately, questions flew everywhere.

"When did this happen?"

"Who's the lucky guy?"

"Is it Carlos?"

"Have you set a date?"

"Where are you going to have the wedding?"

For the next half hour, the other women shared in Melissa's joy.

It doesn't matter whether the diamond is as small as a chip or
so big that it weighs down the finger, an engagement ring is a gorgeous piece of jewelry. It's not the gem that's so beautiful, but all
the symbolism behind the ring. Here's what it signifies:

- The beginning of a new life
- Joining a new family (the inlaws!)
- Changing your name
- Embarking on a new role (wife, and perhaps eventually, mother)
- Having a new place to live; and, most of all
- Gaining a lifelong best friend

If you are married or plan to be married soon, you can empathize with the excitement and joy that a bride-to-be feels. So many things to do. So many plans to make. I remember writing out all those wedding invitations. I wanted the whole world—or at least most of Oklahoma—to know that I was marrying Bill Bright!

We can make a comparison between the joy we felt when we stood at the brink of marriage to one of the other most exciting experiences a Christian can ever have—seeing someone come to know Jesus as Savior and Lord. When I've seen the expression on the face of the person who has just received Christ and realizes that all his or her sins are forgiven, and feels the deep love of Jesus for the first time, I'm thrilled too.

Look at the parallels between the two events. A bride is gaining a new best friend—her husband. When I share my faith in Christ with another woman, I am introducing her to the one Person who will become her eternal best friend. In fact, the Bible describes Jesus as the bridegroom of the Church (see John 3:29). What an apt illustration! What a perfect Bridegroom! He will never leave His bride nor fail her; He will be beside her at every moment of every day.

A bride is embarking on a new way of life. A new believer also begins a brand-new life. Her old ways of sin and defeat are behind her, and now she has the hope that Hebrews 11:1 gives us—that she will one day live forever with Jesus. A bride is also receiving a new name—that of her husband. Along with her new life, the believer receives a new name, Christian. That name links her with the Creator of the universe, Jesus Christ.

On her wedding day, a new bride becomes a part of her husband's extended family. At the moment a person invites Jesus to be his or her Savior, he or she also is ushered in to a new family, God's family. This new believer begins to play a new role as a child of the King.

If you are married, why do you wear a wedding ring? It's to tell the world that you belong to someone, that you have taken vows to be faithful to that person. Your wedding ring is a testimony to your relationship with your husband. As Christians, we also have a testimony to the fact that we belong to Jesus. Our faith is as valuable to us as the most costly diamond! Think of your faith moments as your wedding ring. They are your testimony, your evidence of your relationship with Jesus Christ!

Don't you want every person you know to have the incredible advantage of knowing God and inviting Jesus to be his or her Savior? Bill and I often discussed that if people outside God's kingdom could really see how blessed they would be when they turned from their darkness into God's light, they would come running to Jesus. That's why we dedicated our lives to spreading God's message of love.

The desperate plight of people without Christ is the reason we must have sharing faith. We can't bottle up our good news inside our hearts and hope that somehow our neighbors and work colleagues will hear the message somewhere else.

The young bride at the garden tea was anxious to share her good news. Her heart was so full of her fiancé that she wanted to tell everyone about him. Have you ever watched a young engaged couple walk through the mall? She's so proud to be linked onto his arm! Her actions announce to the world that she loves her soon-to-be husband.

We should be even more excited about sharing our love for Jesus with the world. We are "engaged" to God's Son! In time, when our faith is realized and we arrive in heaven, we will celebrate in the marriage supper of the Lamb. That is the feast when those of us who make up the Church—all the believers of the Church age—will become the Bride of Christ. What a day that will be!

You may be thinking right now: *Sharing my faith is too difficult. I wouldn't know what to say. I don't know the right words.*

That's what this chapter will help you accomplish. You can learn how to simply and clearly communicate to others how much God loves them and how they can find peace and hope in Jesus. The secret is in those faith moments you have experienced.

Sharing Your Faith Through Faith Moments

I firmly believe that as women we have advantages over men in sharing our faith. For the most part, we can connect with each other more easily and quickly. We aren't afraid to express ourselves to another woman on a deeper level than many men are comfortable with. Women have a great capacity to persuade people. Perhaps this comes from the nurturing acts of motherhood and the need to persuade children to eat and sleep.

The Scriptures command us to share our faith, and we're promised the power of the Holy Spirit when we do so (see Acts 1:8). As a new believer, I wanted to tell others about Christ, but I was concerned that I would fail because I wasn't familiar with Scripture.

Then I read 1 John 1:3: "We are telling you about what we ourselves have actually seen and heard, so that you may fellowship with us. And our fellowship is with the Father and with His Son, Jesus Christ." From that verse, I realized that all I had to do was share what I had "seen and heard"—what God had revealed to me up to that point in my life. In other words, I could tell about all those faith moments I'd had! Perhaps a big faith moment from the past that meant so much to me would fit into the conversation, or a small faith moment that I had experienced yesterday would help me begin a conversation about Jesus. Those faith moments were part of the evidence, my testimony, about my relationship with Jesus Christ, the lover of my soul. When I shared these moments as a new believer, I found that many people were looking for the answers that I had found. Even though I didn't know a lot about the Scriptures, people were interested in what had happened to me. Once they began to know about my precious Savior, I could bring them to the Scriptures.

Now, so many years later, I find that all of life's experiences prepare me to share my faith with others. When I am alone with a person for more than five minutes, I make it my practice to pursue a conversation with regard to that person's spiritual interests. I try to identify with her in some way that would give us common ground on which to converse. That's where my faith moments come in so well.

In some situations, time is limited. Then I share the booklet *Beginning Your Journey of Joy* that was designed specifically for women who are not part of the family of God. (I have included the content of the booklet in the back of this book.) I simply read through the booklet with my conversation friend, letting the words explain the simple plan of salvation through Bible verses and illustrations. Not everyone with whom I share my faith will respond, but God only asks me to be faithful to share my faith. He is responsible for the results. And that's all He expects from you.

I have spent more than 50 years sharing my faith. Bill and I and the staff of Campus Crusade have developed excellent training materials and seminars that have helped people all over the world to share their faith. Let me give you some of the truths I've learned along the way.

Share with Boldness

One of the difficulties many Christians have in sharing their faith is that they let fear rule their hearts. But fear is the opposite of faith. Second Timothy 1:7-8 says, "God has not given us a spirit of fear and timidity, but of power, love, and self-discipline. So you must never be ashamed to tell others about our Lord."

I read a story recently that illustrates how the Lord uses those who have a bold witness for Him. Chang Shen was a blind man, 36 years old, who lived in Manchuria in the late 1800s. A violent, hard-drinking man, he was a despised person. One day he heard that some foreign doctors at a hospital 120 miles away might be able to cure his blindness, so he set out alone on a mission to be healed. On the way, people took advantage of him, and he was beaten and robbed. Tragically, when he finally arrived at the hospital, he found out that the beds were full, and he was told to go away.

Where could he go? All he could do was curl up in a doorway to sleep. The night watchman discovered him there and felt pity for him, so he went to the chief of the hospital and offered his own bed to the blind man.

Over the next month, the doctors treated Chang's eyes, and he recovered some of his sight. But when he visited a local Chinese practitioner to find even more sight, the man pierced the pupil of Chang's eye with a needle, which plunged him into total darkness.

But Chang Shen received a different kind of sight. While being treated at the hospital, he heard about the love of Jesus. He became a Christian, and his life completely changed!

After being treated, Chang took some gospel tracts and went back home. As soon as he got back, he began to tell everyone about Jesus. But what an unlikely witness! He had such a bad reputation as a violent man!

Later, a missionary from the hospital traveled to see Blind Chang. When he arrived at the village, he found a thriving, small church.

In 1900, the Boxer Rebellion spread within China. This was an uprising against all foreigners and those who associated with them. Because Christianity was linked to Westerners, Chinese Christians were singled out for persecution. Many were imprisoned.

Chang asked to trade places with some of the believers who were to be executed. On July 22, 1900, Chang was put on a cart designed to transport animals and was driven to his execution. As he went, he sang, "Jesus loves me, this I know, for the Bible tells me so." Just before the sword severed his neck, he cried out, "Heavenly Father, receive my spirit!"

At that moment of faith, not only did he witness to all around him of his love for God, but the first face he likely saw on the other side was that of Jesus!

Probably none of us will need the kind of boldness that God gave Chang, but whatever measure you need, God will provide. Paul writes, "Pray that I will keep on speaking boldly for him, as I should" (Eph. 6:20).

Boldly doesn't mean obnoxiously. Some of the most genteel women I know are the most effective at sharing their faith. They just let the Lord use them as they are—with their own personality traits—to open a spiritual conversation with a faith story that leads to telling the gospel. God has made you to be you, and He will use you just as you are! He has provided you with faith moments that can be your opening to share Jesus with the people you know and meet.

Share in Purity

My life changed dramatically when Bill was diagnosed with pulmonary fibrosis. Our lifestyle changed from going to the office every day to creating a home office environment. As Bill's illness progressed, we had medical people in and out frequently, and in the last months of his life we had full-time nursing care. Not everyone who came into our home was a Christian, and it was so important to me that our faith remained a consistent witness to the glory of God.

Because of Bill's breathing difficulties, it was imperative that we keep the air as free from dust as possible. At one point, we discovered a rather severe problem with mold. This sent us on a wild adventure, to say the least. After an expert evaluation of our home, we were informed that we needed to pull up the carpeting and have all the soft furniture and any fabric surfaces thoroughly cleaned. He also recommended that we install wood floors.

My dear husband was so committed to several writing projects and trying with all his might to keep the Global Pastors Network activities going strong that our home was truly a "Grand Central Station." How would I ever manage to get the floors redone and keep things going? Our dear friend Anne Drexel lives in our building, and she extended an invitation for us to move into her condo during the process of getting the floors redone.

You may remember from an earlier chapter when I explained about the household demands in the early days of our ministry when I began resenting all the work I had to do. Well, here I was again, trying to survive in total chaos. We packed up the absolute bare necessities and moved in with our dear friend and neighbor. The move meant fax and phone lines had to be forwarded, and that was just the beginning of the transition. I was informed that once I left our condo and the construction work began, I could not reenter my home because I would carry particles on me when I returned to Bill.

Do you realize all the spiritual applications I could make from the beginning of this saga until today? I must relate one incident that was so profound. We thought we had identified all the areas of our home that needed attention until one of the staff was looking in a storage closet and discovered a water spot on the interior wall of the closet. You probably guessed it. Behind the wall was a major amount of mold. The wall had to be replaced, so of course this delayed the total project.

That mold hidden in the closet is like the sins we cover up and let fester in the crevices of our lives. Even though we may think they are hidden, they are still infecting our life.

I cannot resist the opportunity to ask you: What do you have hiding in your life that needs to be uncovered and cleaned out? We all have something that God needs to eliminate to make us perfectly clean and whole. The process of staying clean before Him is one of daily confession and trusting the Holy Spirit to indwell us and fill us with His power. To be the most effective witness for Jesus, we must be a clean vessel for Him to use. I think of that closet wall when I come before my Savior to confess my weakness and ask Him to search my heart for any sin that may be growing in my life. This process is spiritual breathing and consistently walking in the power of the Holy Spirit. This is the only way we will become fruitful witnesses for our Lord.

In time, the wood floors were installed and we did return to our home. The air was definitely cleaner, and that added days to Bill's life and most certainly improved the quality of his breathing.

My point in telling you all these details is to help you recognize that sharing your faith is not always a deliberate one-on-one encounter. In those moments when life seems to be crashing in on you, someone may be watching and just waiting to see how your faith impacts how you react to the stresses of life. A neighbor or a relative may be hungry to find spiritual peace, but can't decide if your faith is genuine. Your purity of life and your willingness to walk in the Spirit is the evidence of your faith to that person.

We live in an age when the distinction between right and wrong is becoming increasingly blurred. Our culture has adopted the principle of situational ethics, which proposes that what is morally right varies from person to person and situation to situation. Yet God's standards do not change; they are timeless. God wants you to display His righteousness in your new life. You can do this through faith as you daily throw off your old evil nature and your former way of life and consciously adopt a spiritual renewal of your thoughts and attitudes. You must display a new nature because you are a new person, created in God's likeness.

Share in All Places

I have found that godly women are very resourceful in where they witness. We have so many roles we play—wife, mother, career woman, neighbor, PTA volunteer, carpool driver, and so forth. Each area is a place where you can share your faith moments. Paul writes, "So everywhere we go, we tell everyone about Christ" (Col. 1:28). He practiced what he preached. He spoke of Jesus in the synagogues, in the streets, before high-level officials and even in prison—even when he knew there was a big possibility that he would be beaten or stoned. He considered every place he went to be the place God sent him to spread the good news of Jesus.

When Bill committed his life to Christ, he became passionate about sharing his faith. I believe because he shared his faith so openly and found most people so receptive, he never considered any other lifestyle. Helping to fulfill the Great Commission was his lifelong mission.

That's true for me too. It is important for me to communicate that sharing faith is not about a method, but it is all about a lifestyle. As a Christian woman, your life should reflect the nature of Christ. His mission on earth was to do the will of His Father. Fortunately, because Christ gave His life for us, we can be reconciled to God.

I am a widow today, and that somehow seems strange as I write these words. But I find that I have so many opportunities to share my faith, and I have purposed to use every remaining day of my life to tell as many people as possible about the wonderful love of our Lord and Savior Jesus Christ.

Many widows faithfully serve the ministry of Campus Crusade. Sue Michels is an example of a woman who continues to serve God even though her husband has gone to be with the Lord.

Sue became a Christian through the ministry of Campus Crusade at Eastern Michigan University and then went on a summer project that changed her life. She married Dave Michels following her college graduation, and they joined Crusade staff together.

Sue wanted to be on staff because she did not want to become a complacent Christian. She wanted the Campus Crusade environment where her faith would be stretched and where she would be challenged to grow spiritually. Being in the front lines of ministry has caused her to depend on the Lord and to follow Him faithfully. Following their time at the International School of Theology in California, Sue decided that she really wanted to get back on campus, sharing her faith. (She had been home with three small boys, one a new baby.) Dave offered to stay with the boys one day a week so that she could go on campus, teach a Bible study and share her faith with some key students on campus.

In 1983, the Michelses packed up their household and moved to Moscow to serve with the CoMission for one year, a huge faith stretcher for the whole family. Sue saw one neighbor come to Christ, was able to go into some schools and an orphanage to teach, and led a Bible club for children—all while keeping Dave and their household going in a foreign situation.

Sue admits to experiencing some tension between being a wife and mother and working with the students on campus. (That reminds me of my own feelings years ago.) But she also realized that she needed to depend on God and His power and focus on what He wants, rather than worrying about how others thought she should spend her time. She says, "As I look at being with Campus Crusade for these past 22 years, I have no regrets about my calling. It has been a privilege to be in ministry and to be a part of what God is doing."

I challenge you to look at your schedule as opportunities to share your faith. Let this sharing spring from your relationship and love for Jesus. It doesn't need to be a cumbersome, artificial experience, but just the joy of your faith moments and the beauty of your Lord shining through your words and life.

One place that I firmly believe God would have us share our faith is in our homes. As we learned in the chapter "A Giving Faith," all we have belongs to God. Since He owns it all, He also owns our homes. What would God want you to do with your home? You may live in an efficiency apartment or a modest two-bedroom house or a mansion on an estate. This place is God's gift to you. And this is where you can be most effective in introducing people to Christ and allowing them to experience a vital faith.

A dear friend of mine, Barbara Ball, exemplifies the woman who gives her home over to God to use as He wills. At 29, she was a lonely, negative, shy woman. But today, she's vibrant and excited. She tells a story about how she first used her home to share her faith in a new neighborhood. She discovered that she had become so busy that she wasn't sharing her faith. She says:

> I discovered this when I planned a Christmas coffee at my home. By this time, Howard [my husband] and I had moved from our Arrowhead Springs bungalow into a house that we purchased in San Bernardino [California]. I sent 25 invitations, but only 3 of my neighbors came. True, small groups are fine with the Lord, but my neighbors didn't come because they didn't know me and were apprehensive about what I was doing.
>
> Right then I decided to get to know my neighbors. I asked the Lord what I could do to meet them, and He impressed on me to consider what I do best.
>
> I love to bake bread, so I began taking a loaf to each home and staying to visit. I continued baking and visiting my neighbors until I had built friendship bridges to them....

After two years in that neighborhood, our torrential rainstorms drove mud down from the mountainside, and our entire area was forced to move. We all helped and loved each other. The local newspapers printed an article and photo of my three friends and me praying for our neighbors. The article was called, "And Barbara, We Will Pray for You!" Most important, I was able to witness to many of those neighbors. That's how I began sharing Christ as a way of life!

Barbara is still sharing her faith and using her home as a center for spreading the good news. She has talents in cooking and decorating, which she uses for God's glory. She has been such an encouragement to me.

Other women use their workplace to hold a Bible study at lunchtime or to build friendship bridges with other women. Your church may have evangelistic outreach programs that are designed to help you reach out to others. Ask God to show you what He wants you to do in the places you go every day.

Sharing as a Lifestyle

As Barbara mentioned, sharing our faith should become our lifestyle. We should make it a practice to see other people through God's eyes. He wants them to find eternal joy and peace with Him. That's what we should desire also. When we bring others to Christ, then encourage them to do the same with the people they know, we create a chain of spiritual multiplication that can truly change our world.

The darling young woman, Carolyn, who is my personal assistant, was attending a conference with me. She had told me about her choice to go as a student into a closed country to create opportunities to share Christ with other students. When she moved to that country, she began meeting young women on campus and inviting them to her apartment. She encouraged them to bring a friend. In the two years she was in that country, she saw many women make commitments to Christ and she was thrilled with her experience.

Upon returning to the United States, Carolyn continued to pray for that country and the people she had encountered. Always close to her heart were the faces of those seeking answers and the ones who responded to God's love and forgiveness.

After four years, you can imagine the joy I saw in her face when what some would call a "chance encounter" became a divine appointment. We entered a restaurant and were greeted by a young woman who recognized my assistant. The young woman's nametag was in her native language, and my assistant pronounced it correctly.

The woman said, "I know you. You were the first to share God with me. I was in your apartment three times. What you shared was so wonderful that I could not believe it was true." She went on to share that she had come to America to study. She found housing in the home of a Christian woman who took her to church. In church, she heard the same good news Carolyn had shared. Now she could believe and receive Christ as her Savior and Lord. She was growing in her faith and was so pleased and excited to tell Carolyn what had happened.

What a thrill for me to witness this scenario unfold. I had prayed for students and staff in the closed country, and now I was meeting a person who had benefited from a staff member's ministry. God doesn't always allow us to see the fruit of our prayers or our efforts, but what a thrill when He does!

Developing a lifestyle of sharing your faith means being ready at all times to tell others about Jesus. Paul writes, "Live wisely among those who are not Christians, and make the most of every opportunity. Let your conversation be gracious and effective so that you will have the right answer for everyone" (Col. 4:5-6). That's a strong charge for us to live with the message of Jesus' love on our lips and in our actions.

Nothing will reward you more than obeying God in the area of sharing your faith. In our next chapter, we will learn how God rewards those who are faithful through faith. We not only have the privilege of serving a God who loves us so much, but He rewards us when we do! I can't imagine a more loving, faithful God!

A Pathway to Deepen My Faith

1. Learning from the Chapter
Think of a time when you enjoyed participating in the wedding of a dear friend. How did you feel? Now think back to when you received Jesus as your Savior. How did you feel? How were the two times similar? How were they different?

_____

_____

_____

_____

_____

_____

What faith moments have you experienced that you could share with someone who doesn't know Jesus? Ask God to lead you to someone who would be open to hearing about your walk with God.

_____

_____

_____

_____

_____

_____

2. Knowing God's Word
The Scripture in Acts 1:8 is the last command Jesus gave us before He ascended to heaven. Write out what it means to you.

_____

_____

_____

_____

_____

_____

Matthew 28:18-20 is the same command as given in Acts 1:8. What does it mean that God will give you power to share your faith or witness for Him?

_____

_____

_____

_____

_____

_____

_____

3. Applying God's Word
The four instructions on how to share our faith are:

1. Share with boldness
2. Share in purity
3. Share in all places
4. Share as a lifestyle

Which one is most difficult for you?

_____

_____

_____

_____

_____

Read the following verses. After each one, write how it encourages you to follow the four instructions for sharing your faith:

2 Timothy 1:7-8 (with boldness)

_____

_____

_____

_____

_____

_____

Colossians 1:28 (in all places)

_____
_____
_____
_____
_____

2 Corinthians 6:6-7 (with purity)

_____
_____
_____
_____
_____

Colossians 4:5-6 (as a lifestyle)

_____
_____
_____
_____
_____

Write down three people in your life that you want to introduce to the truth about Jesus. Pray for them daily and ask God to give you opportunities to share your faith with them.

_____
_____
_____
_____
_____

Become familiar with "Beginning Your Journey of Joy" at the end of the book so that when the opportunities to share your faith come, you will be ready.

9

A Rewarding Faith

*Now when Christ says: make to yourselves friends, lay up for
yourselves treasures, and the like, you see that he means: do good,
and it will follow itself without your seeking, that you will have friends,
find treasures in heaven, and receive a reward.*

MARTIN LUTHER

Janice worked in an office where the rewards were nonexistent. Yes, she got a regular paycheck and it was adequate for her needs, but the office atmosphere lent itself to a feeling of defeatism and worthlessness. A recent incident was so indicative of how her boss ran the department. Janice had arrived at the point where she wasn't sure she wanted to even work in this place anymore. She had even dusted off her résumé!

It had culminated like this. She and three of the employees in her area had been assigned to work on the big budget report. The instructions were to highlight areas of loss that could be targeted for reduction. The four of them had done a thorough job, spending extra hours on the report, but that overtime was not reflected in their paychecks. Their findings were complete and professional.

But then their department head reprimanded the four of them for issuing bad news in certain areas of the budget. She argued with their conclusions, saying that they were trying to undermine her reputation as a supervisor. When they tried to explain how the budget shortfalls could be corrected and how that would help the bottom line, she just tossed the report back at them.

A week later, Janice found out that the supervisor had asked one of her "pet" employees to come up with a new report. This man put together a superficial, glowing report that didn't address any of the problems. And he looked good! Janice and her colleagues felt like they were being blackballed from any more high-level decision-making.

Because of the supervisor's actions, the morale in the office plummeted. All the employees pulled back, making sure they didn't go against the supervisor's wishes, even when their actions hurt the progress in the office.

Compare this office with the atmosphere in Pam's company. Her boss is scrupulously fair. He gets to know his employees and tries to assign tasks that fit best with their skills and talents. He consistently compliments people on their extra efforts at work and also recognizes when someone is not pulling his or her own share of the workload. Pam feels comfortable raising sticky issues because she knows she'll get a fair hearing. She remembers the day when she complained about a colleague, June, who was spending lots of work time doing personal telephone calling, creating a bottleneck for Pam's work. The result of this woman's idle time was that Pam's area of responsibility was suffering. Pam had tried to resolve the problem, but June just brushed her off and continued her behavior.

Pam's boss listened to Pam's problem, then discreetly handled the issue, and things improved. Pam felt really good about being heard over a legitimate complaint.

None of us like to work in a place where we are not fairly treated or rewarded. We thrive best when we are assured that what we do is noticed.

That's one aspect of our faith that's so reassuring. We serve a God who is completely fair and loving. Whatever we do for Him will result in all kinds of blessings and rewards. We never have to worry that He is too busy to notice our actions or that He will misrepresent what we do. He sees all, including our heart and motives, and loves to reward us for what we do for Him. He treats us as His sons and daughters, not just as hired hands or servants.

We do not bargain with God. We serve Him out of love, compassion and obedience, expecting nothing in return.

As we get to know our God in a deeper relationship, we will see even more His great love and devotion to us. He is interested in every detail of our lives. He remembers our good works.

Hebrews 11:6 says, "Anyone who wants to come to him must believe that there is a God and that he rewards those who sincerely seek him." In other words, our faith in God brings us blessings from the hand of God.

The Bible describes God as an employer who pays fair wages to His workers. As we labor for Him, He records what we do and then gives back to us in even greater measure. We may not always see immediate payment for what we do, but God never forgets. This world is not fair, and we will not get fair treatment from the enemy of our soul—Satan—but God is always fair and is beside us at all times.

The rewards for our faith come at two different times. First, we receive certain rewards for following Jesus in this life. These rewards include the good consequences of living according to the way that God designed us. Later, when we meet Jesus in heaven, He will reward us for our good deeds at His judgment seat. Ephesians 6:8 promises, "Remember that the Lord will reward each one of us for the good we do, whether we are slaves or free." And Jeremiah 17:10 says, "But I know! I, the LORD, search all hearts and examine secret motives. I give all people their due rewards, according to what their actions deserve." These are promises from God!

Are you excited about what God has in store for you? Are you already experiencing His blessings for your faith? Let's look at some of the areas in which we will see the rewards of our faith.

Receiving Peace and Joy

One of the here-and-now rewards we receive for our faith is experiencing God's peace and joy. This comes no matter what our circumstances may be. That's what I discovered during that faith moment early in my Christian life at the time when I felt so dissatisfied and unfulfilled with my roles as wife, mother and partner in the ministry.

Around that time, Bill began to emphasize 1 Thessalonians 5:18 in his teaching. Though I had heard it many times—"In everything give thanks; for this is God's will for you in Christ Jesus" (NASB)—I decided to begin to apply the verse. I began to thank God for everything—for dishwashing, dinner preparation, interruptions, people and the many tedious tasks I had to do.

In the beginning, I didn't find it easy to give thanks. Many times, through tears, I tried to practice what I had learned. Inevitably, the most difficult time to apply these new truths occurred every Tuesday night.

In our home we held meetings for college students at which a message about Jesus Christ would be given. Bill and the staff living with us would move all the furniture out of the way, and students would jam-pack the dining room, the two halls, the living room and up into a little room that served as a study.

Most of the time while the students were there, I had to be in the kitchen getting the refreshments, and I resented it terribly. I wanted to be in the forefront as the hostess—helping to make the announcements, introducing the students and talking to them personally about Jesus Christ. Many times, as I was getting the refreshments, I would complain, *Now, Lord, I could lead these students to Christ in half the time these new staff members could. They ought to be in here getting these refreshments, and I ought to be out there.*

Yet, in my heart, I knew that this was right. They needed the training, so I tried to apply my new truth. I prayed: *Thank You, Father, for the privilege of getting these refreshments. Thank You that I can serve You in this kitchen. I may not meet one student tonight, but thank You for the privilege of preparing these refreshments for them.*

Little by little, I began to experience real joy—God-given joy—in preparing the punch and the cookies for Him. After that, I began to do everything for the Lord. I washed diapers for Jesus. I mopped floors for Jesus. I cleaned house for Jesus—not for Campus Crusade, not for Bill Bright, not for Henrietta Mears, not for my family—but I was doing it for Jesus. It amazed me to gradually see the drudgery and the humdrum work turn into activities that had meaning and new purpose. I started in a new way to use the creative mind God had given me, and I began to get organized.

After a few weeks, the house was running like clockwork. God had sent enough domestic help to relieve me of some of the responsibility. At the same time, I found I could do more than one task at a time. By changing my negative attitude, I gained creative energy I hadn't known I possessed. I truly began to enjoy my home, to accept it as my ministry, and I was challenged to reach my greatest personal potential right there.

Often when students came for counseling, they would say, "Isn't there something I can do to help?" I found I could mend clothes or sew on buttons, and they could iron handkerchiefs or tablecloths while I counseled with them. If I were getting dinner, I'd invite them into the kitchen and continue to prepare my meals as I was counseling. Of course, there were times when that was not appropriate; however, by allowing them to help, they felt like they were a greater part of my life. Talking and sharing with each other was even more casual and meaningful as we worked together. When they offered to help, I learned to accept their help. I soon had more time to be on the campus working with the students than when I had full-time help at home.

What was the difference? My attitude had changed. I had learned that the Lord was my source of joy, peace and happiness—not my circumstances, nor the way people treated me.

The reason I can now say that my joy is in the Lord is that I know that wherever He puts me, I can be the most productive. Even in this time of adjusting to a life without Bill, the Lord has given me incredible peace and joy. Yes, the sorrow and loss are still sharp and painful, but my life is still so rich with Jesus. Because I know I am doing exactly what He wants me to do, I can experience great satisfaction and joy. That's the kind of reward for my faith that the world can never give. You will experience this reward also as you put your faith into practice.

I can't adequately tell you the thrill that is mine to be approached almost daily as I am recognized or introduced as Mrs. Bill Bright, and people make a point of coming to me to share,

"Your husband led me to Christ" or "I found Christ while on the campus [of some university or college] through Campus Crusade."

I was ready to give my editor the final edits on this book when, just before calling her, I picked up my mail. The envelope I was holding in my hand stopped me in my steps. I ran my finger over the return address and paused for a moment of praise and reflection at what those few letters spelling out a name meant to me. There it was, Nancy Moore, not an unusual name, but this letter was from a very unusual woman.

Nancy entered UCLA School of Nursing as a sophomore and was totally committed to becoming a nurse. Her parents were not believers; however, something in Nancy's past, perhaps the influence of a grandparent, motivated her to want to do something "good," and to her that meant something religious. There was a nondenominational organization on the UCLA campus; so Nancy went to find out what she could do. She was told by the lady at the desk that there was nothing for her to do. Obviously, this was a disappointment to Nancy, eager to serve.

Two weeks later, she was invited to a Campus Crusade meeting where she heard athletes and sorority girls share their experiences with Christ. I approached Nancy at the conclusion of the meeting and asked her some very basic questions:

- Did you like the information you heard?
- Did this make sense to you?
- Have you ever done anything about asking Christ into your life?
- Would you like to find out more?

Nancy responded with a definite yes.

I told Nancy I would pick her up five days later and we would talk again. Nancy has expressed to me the great anticipation she felt waiting for our conversation. So that day, in the warm California sun, sitting in my car, Nancy eagerly accepted Jesus Christ as her personal savior. We prayed! I remember her delight as she defined herself as "a brand-new person." We met weekly, and

Nancy began to memorize Scripture and grow in her faith-walk with Christ.

Nancy has told me that when she told her parents, they calmly informed her, "It's okay; it will pass."

In Nancy's junior year she transferred to UC Berkeley to pursue her nursing education. She found a great church. After her fourth year in college she attended a College Briefing sponsored by Hollywood Presbyterian Church with Miss Mears at Forest Home, in the California mountains. There she met the man who would become the love of her life. Mark wanted to be a pastor, and when they married, Nancy worked to help put him through seminary. Mark had been a Navy pilot; so for them to go to Brazil as missionaries and Mark to work as a bush pilot was not a surprise to those who knew them well.

After 10 years of service in Brazil, Mark and Nancy returned home and left the work in the capable hands of Brazilian nationals.

Mark and Nancy now serve a local congregation, Mark as an assistant pastor and Nancy as parish nurse care.

Nancy has three daughters, and all are committed Christian women, one serving for over 20 years in a hostile foreign country. I recently learned that the next generation is also committed to Christian service and a grandson is preparing to return to Brazil.

When I saw the return address on that envelope, Nancy's life story flooded my thoughts with gratitude for her life. Nancy was the first person I led to Christ on the UCLA campus, and her note to me that day was on the fifty-sixth anniversary of her new birth in Christ, just to say thanks.

How can anything compare with the rewards of a life of faith?

Receiving God's Guidance

If you are like me, sometimes you just don't know what to do or where to turn. Difficult choices in life arise. You may have to choose between two excellent options that are very different and that you know will lead to very separate results. Whether to accept this job or that one. Which ministry option would be most effective. Which college to attend. Other times, your way is just not clear. You've been laid off from your job and you can't find a new one. Your son or daughter is failing at school and you don't know how to change the trend. Those living in the world must rely on whatever good sense or information they have at the time, but we have something in our grasp that far exceeds any human resource—God's guidance. Our faith gives us access to that guidance.

God gives us much assurance from His Word that He is in control of our circumstances. In Philippians 2:13 we learn, "It is God who is at work in you, both to will and to work for His good pleasure" (*NASB*). I have come to realize that as I submit my will to the Lord, He is not going to allow me to make a mistake. If He plants in me the desire to accomplish a task, He will also give me the power to do it.

In one of the guiding verses of my life, Psalm 37:5, we are told, "Commit your way to the LORD. Trust also in Him, and He will do it" (*NASB*). The first seven verses of Psalm 37 give us these clear directions and encouragement: Don't fret because of evildoers; don't worry, or actually, stop worrying; delight in the Lord and He'll give you the desires of your heart. Also, in Proverbs 3:5-6, we are told, "Lean not unto thine own understanding. In all thy ways acknowledge him, and he shall direct thy paths" (*KJV*). These verses of Scripture have been a mainstay to me as I have trusted Him to guide me in the right direction.

I have learned that when I look at my circumstances, it is easy to become discouraged and defeated, for I am not making myself available to God. But Scripture tells us the solution: "Set your mind on the things above, not on the things that are on earth. For you have died and your life is hidden with Christ in God" (Col. 3:2-3, *NASB*). I realize from these verses that I am to look to Christ in every kind of situation—to set my sights and my affections on Him, and then I will have victory. This is faith in action.

Applying this concept became real when guests arrived unexpectedly in the midst of an overloaded daily schedule. After seating her guests, Miss Mears would often appear at the spot where I was working and say, "Honey, would you mind serving a little pot of tea to the committee meeting?"

Many times I had happily replied, "I'd love to," but in my heart I was saying (ashamedly now), *Why doesn't she get her own cup of tea?* But when I allowed God to guide all my circumstances, big and little, I was able to genuinely say, "I would be happy to serve you tea," no matter what the inconvenience, because I was available to God.

Another example is the many times when demands of the ministry would change Bill's or my schedule at the last moment. These were hard for me to accept because I like to live with structure. But I would just look to the Lord and say, "It's Your time, God. I'll do with it what You want me to do." Always I would soon see the good results of letting God have His way.

We determine in our own minds whether or not we are going to be upset and how we are going to react to a situation. Jesus said, "Let not your heart be troubled. You are trusting God, now trust in me" (John 14:1, *TLB*). When disappointing news comes, we must strive to develop the habit of quickly saying to the Lord, "I trust You. I will not let my heart be troubled."

But what about those gigantic situations that loom like the sinking Titanic on your horizon? How can we handle them? Often people say, "Don't tell me about saying thank you to God for a situation or a circumstance in life. You don't have the problems I have." That was what one woman remarked to a friend of mine, Charissa, who was teaching a class on the principle of God's perfect plan for our lives. Janice became very critical of Charissa's assurance that God is always in control.

Charissa quizzed Janice and learned that she was bitter because her husband was dying of cancer. Charissa explained to her student how God had worked uniquely in her own life when her own husband had died a few years before. She told how her husband had prayed that after he died God would bring her a loving Christian man who would be a good husband to her and a good father to her nine-year-old son. Of course, Charissa wasn't interested in another person then and only wanted her husband to be well. Yet, a few years after his death, God sent a loving Christian man into her life who desired to enter Christian work, which had also been her desire.

She now had a second husband, who was the absolute delight of her life and a tremendous father to her son. God had also given her the opportunity to teach others the reality of God in their personal lives. Janice was stunned to think she was talking to someone who had gone through a circumstance similar to hers and had seen God use that in her life for good.

I'll never forget the words of Dale Evans Rogers (wife of the famous movie cowboy, Roy Rogers) as she spoke at a congressional wives' prayer breakfast. Her daughter, Debbie, had been killed in a bus accident, and this was Dale's first speaking engagement since the accident. We were all concerned about Dale and Roy, and grieved with them, but she victoriously opened her remarks with, "Ladies, I'm here to tell you that God is real. I know." From that moment on, everyone knew that what Dale had to say about God she had experienced through her sorrow. God used that tragedy in Dale's life to touch the hearts of so many other women around the world. I don't know all the reasons why God allowed this terrible death to happen in Dale's family, but I do know that God comforted and guided Dale and Roy through their time of sorrow. Dale's attitude of thankfulness to God in spite of her sorrow certainly ministered to all of us that day.

God will do the same for you. Our faith opens our hearts to knowing what God has planned for us. We have the direct commands in God's Word that will shape our actions as we study and apply it. In addition, through prayer, God will lead you in your life's pathway. God will never leave you friendless. You can count on Him!

Building a New Character

So many times we want to escape the character building that God wants to perform in our lives. We would like to take shortcuts to becoming the total person God wants us to be. We would like to escape the difficulties, and yet God sees our faith as a way to build character in our lives that will allow us to become more and more like Jesus.

Trying circumstances are teaching ground. As we face unpleasant difficulties and situations, God is giving us a message that we can share with others. Many times we would like to be of help to other people; we would like to have an outstanding ministry. But before we can have a ministry, we must have a message. How do we develop a message? By experiencing the reality of God in all kinds of situations. And so, even though we don't ask for them, as unpleasant and hard times come, we can learn to thank God because He will use them to our betterment. He will take those circumstances, which may seem tragic, chaotic and frustrating through human eyes, and make them into meaningful and constructive experiences. He will use them to conform us to the image of Christ and make us into the person we desire to be.

As long as we resist God's will or remain bitter, discouraged and angry, God cannot do His work in our lives. But as we submit to Him and thank Him, we are able to learn the lessons He wants us to know. This is a giant step toward becoming fulfilled as Christians.

Jesus does this by coming alongside to help us. He's right by our side, showing us what to do and encouraging us to develop traits that honor God.

His work with us reminds me of an incident that happened on April 28, 2003. The Portland Trail Blazers were playing a nationally televised NBA Western Conference playoff game that Friday night. Thirteen-year-old Natalie Gilbert was selected to sing "The Star-Spangled Banner." As the crowd that packed Portland's Rose Garden Arena stood in excitement and anticipation, she took her place alone at midcourt. She belted out the first few lines, then somewhere around the "twilight's last gleaming," she forgot the words. She closed her eyes and shook her head. She appeared to be on the verge of tears. Desperate, Gilbert turned to look for her father. That's when she saw the Trail Blazers' coach Maurice Cheeks walking toward her. The coach put his arm around the girl and began singing with her. He encouraged the crowd to sing along. Together, they made it all the way through to "the home of the brave."

"I didn't even know if I knew all the words, but as many times as I've heard the national anthem, I just went over and continued to sing," the coach told CBS SportsLine later. "The words started coming back to me and I just tried to help her out."

"It helped me a lot. It made me feel more comfortable," Natalie said in a CNN interview. "It was just like having a huge choir of 20,000 people around you just singing a great patriotic song."

Natalie needed help, and the coach responded. You may feel like Natalie when you are in a situation that is out of your control or above your ability. But wherever you find yourself, God will reward you for your service. He will walk beside you and put His arm around you to help you. Whatever you are facing, He will help you overcome and build that spiritual character that He desires to see in your life. You will become more whole and fulfilled, and you will not feel alone.

Receiving Physical Benefits

The concept of a "makeover" has always been intriguing to me. Television programs offer contests where people submit requests for someone they feel deserves a makeover. A recent primetime network special featured a makeover for men and women. I am not certain how the participants were selected, but in each case, someone had written in telling the story of the person she thought should be selected.

Some of the makeover processes included delicate surgeries and major dental work. When the moment came to present the person in his or her new form, photographs labeled "before" were shown, the person made a grand entrance, and then "after" photos were displayed alongside the "before" photos. The contrast was usually quite dramatic. Usually, the "before" photo face was somber and seldom smiling, contrasted against the "after" photo projecting a smile and twinkling eyes.

As Christians, we have "before" and "after" pictures. Do you remember what you were like before you came to faith in Christ Jesus? The changes are even more dramatic than those "before" and "after" makeover photos. These spiritual changes are reflected not only in our spirits, but they also have an effect on our bodies.

Up to this point, we have pointed out the spiritual rewards that occur in our walk with God, but amazingly, when we live by faith, the rewards also build up our physical life. For many years, our medical community tried to eliminate spiritual emphasis from the medical field. They felt that a patient's belief in God was so personal that it shouldn't be brought into the hospital and clinic. They even discounted any positive benefits that prayer or faith may have on wellness or recovery. The emphasis was on the "miracles" that science could obtain through medical techniques. But now even medical scientists are realizing that a person's spiritual welfare has a lot to do with his or her physical welfare.

In a *Newsweek* article titled "Why Religion Helps," the magazine reports that religion promotes longer life, protects against cardiac disease and improves recovery rates. Regularly attending church also adds to the quality of life, including less depression and a healthier lifestyle.

These results just make sense to me. What does God emphasize? Getting along with your neighbor. Loving each other. Forgiving others. Finding relief from guilt through Jesus Christ. All these actions promote good health. The Bible warns against activities that would hurt us: worry, drunkenness, sexual impurity, and other sins. After all, God is the One who created us. He has planned our lives for our good. He has written the owner's manual for living—the Bible. When we follow His instruction manual, we are healthier.

When we get into trouble, He has His arms open wide to bring us back and comfort us. When life seems against us, He is for us, standing up with us and showing us that He is in control.

First Chronicles 29:11-12 says, "Yours, O LORD, is the greatness, the power, the glory, the victory, and the majesty. Everything in the heavens and on earth is yours, O LORD, and this is your kingdom. We adore you as the one who is over all things. Riches and honor come from you alone, for you rule over everything. Power and might are in your hand, and it is at your discretion that people are made great and given strength."

Our reward for faith comes from submitting our will to His will and living according to His directions. That will give us the added benefit of physical strength and longevity. Having faith isn't a magic pill that vaccinates us from all illness, but our spiritual good health does have a direct reward in increasing our ability to live in physical good health.

Getting Along with Others

When Melody bought her first used car, she was young and didn't realize how essential it is to maintain the engine and other parts, like tires and brakes. She just kept running the car, fixing whatever broke and then running it again. Within a few years, her car had major engine problems. Eventually, they became so costly that they were more expensive to fix than the car was worth. She had to sell her car to a junk dealer and start all over. When she bought her next car, the first thing she did was consult the owner's manual and set up routine maintenance visits with the repair shop.

Can you see a parallel with Melody's situation and how we treat our relationships with other people, especially those we love most? We don't think about it this way, but all relationships take regular "maintenance." As I look around our world today, I notice that much of the conflict arises from the fact that people don't get along. Graphic examples can be found on the many court programs on television. The judges are mainly presiding over arguments between ex-spouses, former friends, hostile relatives and disgruntled neighbors.

One reward we will experience when we live by faith is that we will learn how to relate to people the way God does—in love, kindness and compassion. The book of Proverbs is filled with practical advice on how to get along with others. In the New Testament, God gives us guidelines on how to perform our roles as wife and mother or employee.

The Bible gives us good methods of conflict resolution and tells us how to deal with personality traits such as a temper that interferes with good personal relationships. Scripture tells us how to handle ourselves when people hurt us or abuse us. And God gives us an eternal perspective on the worth of the people in our lives.

The Bible is the best source for promoting healthy relationships. When we follow its guidelines, we will see improvements in our parenting skills, work habits, word choices and all actions toward others. Of course, we will occasionally find ourselves in situations where the gospel brings about division, because God tells us that we are in a spiritual battle. I think of the young woman who was harassed by a coworker because she simply had a Bible on her desk. We are to expect to face persecutions for the name of our Lord. But we can avoid actions, words or manners that would give cause for people to be antagonistic toward us. Remember the old adage: Honey draws more flies than vinegar. But in most of our relationships, we will find that our reward for getting along with others is peace with others when we walk by faith.

As you search God's Word and apply its instructions to your life, you will find other rewards in this life. I have just mentioned a few. But the real rewards come later, when we meet Jesus face to face.

Rewards that Come Later

What a thrill it is to watch the Olympics! Here we can see an athlete from a small country step up onto a platform to receive a gold medal for being the best at his or her sport while the whole world watches. Perhaps her name is impossible for most people to pronounce. Maybe he's never set foot outside his corner of the world. But here they are, being honored for their physical abilities. It doesn't matter if they're rich or poor, handsome or not so handsome; the medal is purely for what they've accomplished. The applause from the packed stadium thunders as the medal is hung around the athlete's neck. Then everyone stands in honor as his or her national anthem is played and his or her country's flag rises over the dais. How many times have we seen tears flow down the cheeks of the grateful winner?

Although the Olympic Games generate lots of controversies during the contests, for the most part, the athletes rewarded are those who perform the best. In some races, that may mean edging out an opponent by a fraction of a second.

We will have an even greater time of reward when we all see Jesus. All the believers throughout the Church age will stand to be recognized for what they have done. But in this contest, no one will raise any controversies or claim he wasn't treated fairly. Each of us individually will stand before the bema, or judgment seat of Christ.

Many Christians mistakenly think that once they receive Christ as their Savior, what they do from then on won't affect their eternal future. After all, God assures them of a place in heaven. It's true that our sins have all been cast into the deepest sea and God will never bring them back to accuse us. But we must also remember that God is going to test what we do in this life. Jesus will reward us for what we do in faith, and we will suffer loss for living in disobedience to God's commands. Paul writes:

> Our aim is to please him always, whether we are in this body or away from this body. For we must all stand before Christ to be judged. We will each receive whatever we deserve for the good or evil we have done in our bodies (2 Cor. 5:9-10).

This judgment is different and separate from the judgment seat of God that unbelievers must face. That is where their eternal doom is pronounced and their sentence of death is carried out. We, as God's children, will never have to face that terrifying moment!

But we will have to give an account of what we did for Jesus (see Rom. 14:10). Paul describes this accounting as a test by fire. All that you have done—all your good and bad deeds—will be piled up like a stacked bonfire. The pile will be lit, and it will roar up with great tongues of flame. When the fire dies down, everyone will see what's left in the ashes. All the bad deeds will have burned up like wood, hay and straw. But everything done in Jesus' name will survive and be purified like molten gold. Paul writes:

> For no one can lay any other foundation than the one we already have—Jesus Christ. Now anyone who builds on that foundation may use gold, silver, jewels, wood, hay, or straw. But there is going to come a time of testing at the judgment day to see what kind of work each builder has done. Everyone's work will be put through the fire to see whether or not it keeps its value. If the work survives the fire, that builder will receive a reward. But if the work is burned up, the builder will suffer great loss (1 Cor. 3:11-15).

Whatever you have built on your faith in Christ will survive the fire test. These are the gold, silver and jewels of your good works. There they will sparkle at the foot of Jesus' throne for Him to see. They will be the basis for the rewards He will give you to enjoy for eternity.

Bruce Wilkinson, founder of Walk Thru the Bible Ministries, describes the moment at the judgment seat of Christ:

> Friend, join me in living wholeheartedly for a day of celebration, not disappointment, at the bema. No reward on earth will compare to the pleasure of seeing unclouded joy on the face of our Savior as He reviews the work of our lives, then leans forward to favor us with the reward He most wants to give. . . . At that moment, when we finally and completely see and understand all that God has done for us and in us and through us—and we know fully that without Him we could not have even one commendable work for Him—our overwhelming response will be to cry out in thanks and praise to Him.[1]

Will you receive the full reward for your good deeds in faith? We read in 2 John 8, "Watch out, so that you do not lose the prize for which we have been working so hard. Be diligent so that you will receive your full reward."

Don't be concerned about what others think about your service for God. He will judge your heart and motives. First Corinthians 4:5 assures us, "When the Lord comes, He will bring our deepest secrets to light and will reveal our private motives. And then God will give to everyone whatever praise is due." Just obey God in faith. That's all He asks.

Imagine yourself on that day before Christ's throne. If you have been faithful to God, Jesus will reward you and heap praises on you for what you have done in His name. That will be an even greater reward than all the rest. An athlete's experience of receiving a medal on a worldwide stage cannot compare with receiving Jesus' "Well done, my good and faithful servant" (Matt. 25:21). You will be standing before the Creator of the universe when He tenderly and lovingly says your name.

It's hard for me to describe just how wonderful God's faith plan is to me. He saved me when I was totally undeserving, drawing me to

Him when I was His enemy. Now He gives me power through His Holy Spirit to do good deeds I couldn't do on my own. Then at the end of time, He will reward me for doing what only He could enable me to do. What an awesome God He is!

Can you see why our faith sparkles so beautifully with all its facets? It reflects the glory of God. Our faith walk is an adventure like no other. But this isn't the end of the story. Our faith walk is taking us somewhere—and when we arrive, we will find the Source of the joy and satisfaction in our souls!

A Pathway to Deepen My Faith

1. Learning from the Chapter
Read Ephesians 6:8. How does this verse challenge your faith? Be specific.

How does it feel to know that Jesus is the One who will reward you for your good deeds?

Meditate on 1 Thessalonians 5:18. How does the following statement from the chapter relate to this verse? "The reason I can now say that my joy is in the Lord is that I know that wherever He puts me, I can be the most productive."

2. Knowing God's Word

Read Psalm 139:23-24. As you complete the study section of this chapter, ask God to search your heart and reveal any hurtful way.

_____

_____

_____

_____

Read the following verses. How does each one show you how to receive guidance from God for building your faith?

Psalm 37:5

_____

_____

_____

_____

Proverbs 3:5-6

_____

_____

_____

_____

_____

Colossians 3:2-3

_____

_____

_____

_____

_____

John 14:1

_____

_____

_____

_____

3. Applying God's Word

Fear is the opposite of faith. How can Psalm 118:6 help you build faith rather than fear?

_____

_____

_____

_____

_____

What kinds of physical benefits do you think you will receive by deepening your faith? See the following verses.

Psalm 118:6

_____

_____

_____

_____

2 Corinthians 5:10

_____

_____

_____

_____

Using the promises in 2 Corinthians 5:10, explain how you will use the fact that your good deeds will be rewarded to help you share your faith with your unbelieving friends.

_____

_____

_____

_____

_____

Note

1. Bruce Wilkinson, *Secrets of the Vine: Breaking Through to Abundance* (Sisters, OR: Multnomah Publishers, 2006).

10

A Hope Realized

Faith sees the invisible, believes the unbelievable,
and receives the impossible.
CORRIE TEN BOOM

As I knew it would, the day came when I had to say the final good-bye to my beloved husband and release him to his eternal reward of dwelling in the presence of the Savior he loved and served. At 7:00 P.M., Bill's breathing had slowed to 11 breaths a minute and was continuing to drop. I asked everyone who was in our home to come into the bedroom, and we began to sing hymns around Bill's bed. We had intermittently been singing for him at his request for the past two or three weeks. He had chosen some of his favorite hymns.

Bill had the slightest tinge of a smile on the right side of his mouth and looked contented and restful. We talked to him and read Scripture to him as long as he seemed to listen. My last reading to him was the love chapter, 1 Corinthians 13, one of his favorites.

When Bill's breaths became 4½ per minute, I knew it wouldn't be long before he left me. I noticed that his brow was smooth, without a sign of stress. I expressed my love for him. As I had cared for him in the last weeks, "my precious angel" had become my most frequently used name for him. As I said those words, I could tell that he was aware of my presence. At that moment, I felt led to say to him, "I want you to go be with Jesus; you want to go be with Jesus, and Jesus wants you to come to Him. Why don't you let Him carry you to heaven?"

I looked away for a moment and looked back, expecting the next breath. It didn't come; he was gone. He was experiencing that realization of faith for which he had lived for so long. He was seeing Jesus face to face, worshiping the One he had served since his early twenties. Even though I ached for him to be here with me, I knew in my deepest core that he was where he was most content and fulfilled. This was the moment for him when the evidence of his faith was assured.

By noon the following day, I was on my way to Colorado to be with the Campus Crusade staff. Once again, I would be surrounded by young people who had dedicated their lives to serving Christ. It was like a homecoming of my own. What greater reward for me than to be with those who shared Bill's vision and will continue to live out the Great Commission! I knew Bill would be pleased.

My heart still aches each time I relive that moment when I lost my life's partner. Yet even in this difficult trial, I can see beyond the pain to the glory that is in store for us in the near future. When Paul writes to the believers in the Colossian church, he commends them for how they lived out their faith. He says, "You do this because you are looking forward to the joys of heaven—as you have been ever since you first heard the truth of the Good News" (Col. 1:5). The joys of heaven mean more to me now than they ever did before. I'm feeling like Paul. I'm anxious to see Jesus, to touch His hands and His feet, and to tell Him how much I love Him—and I will be reunited with Bill. Right now, I am still content to stay here on this earth to finish the tasks that He has given me to do (see 2 Cor. 4:16–5:10).

You and I hold in our hands the diamond of faith. It is so precious and delicate, yet so indestructible. We have discovered many elements of our faith that we can practice in our lives:

- *A Knowing Faith*—We get to know God and the wonder of His nature.
- *A Living Faith*—We live each moment through the power of His Holy Spirit.
- *A Serving Faith*—We use our God-given power to help others.
- *A Giving Faith*—We use our God-given resources to build God's kingdom.

- *A Sharing Faith*—We spread our faith in Jesus to others.
- *A Rewarding Faith*—We rest in the assurance that God will bless us for our faith.

You may be just beginning your journey of faith, or you may be like me and can see the end of the road in sight. Either way, faith is what sustains us, encourages us and builds our faith.

I would like you to take what I have shared with you in this book to give you the same hope that has given me such joy and fulfillment over these years. If you just keep on going, you will see the realization of your faith! God is not asking you to live a perfect Christian life, just to place your hand in His and walk beside Him. He will help you over the bumpy places and guide you around the dangerous spots. He will help you stay true to your faith when the "good" things of this world try to lure you away. He will show you more beauty than you ever expected. Then He will bring you home to the realization of your faith.

Let me give you a few parting truths that you can use to help you in your walk by faith.

Truths About Our Faith

One thing I have learned through the years is that when things look the bleakest, God is working His greatest miracles. Many times we can't see what He's doing, but He has a way of stretching our faith and giving us hope when the storm clouds lift.

In 1818, a crisis was brewing in Oberndorf, Austria, a tiny alpine village. Josef Mohr was the new village priest, and the church organ had broken down. It was December 23, and the next day he was expected to hold the Christmas Eve liturgical service. How could the people worship without their magnificent organ? But a repairman couldn't be hired until after Christmas Day. He didn't know what to do.

At the time, a roving band of actors was performing in towns throughout the Austrian Alps. Because the church organ was out of commission, the actors presented their Christmas drama in a private home. The amateur actors put on a beautiful re-creation of the simple birth of Christ. After watching the presentation, Mohr was moved by the play and decided to take a longer route home. The longer path took him up a hill overlooking the village.

As Mohr watched the lights twinkle in the distance and took in the majestic silence of that winter night, he began to reflect on a poem that he had written several years earlier in 1816. The poem, which he called "Stille Nacht," was about the night when angels announced the birth of the Messiah to the shepherds who watched their flocks on a hillside. Mohr thought that the words for his poem might make a good carol for the congregation to sing at the Christmas Eve service.

The next morning, Mohr took the poem to his organist, Franz Gruber, who quickly wrote a melody for the hymn that he could play on his guitar. That Christmas Eve, instead of the resounding tones of a magnificent organ, the sweet melody of a guitar, a girls' choir and the two men debuted the song we know today as "Silent Night." Its message and melody are still touching hearts today. But it was born through the agony of a young priest's crisis. What a faith moment!

Doesn't this story illustrate the wonders of our faith? God works in the midst of the darkest times. And God's glory sparkles in the midst of our lives like a diamond on a velvet background.

In an ad in a newspaper for a Beverly Hills jewelry store, the caption under the photo of a gorgeous diamond ring reads, "Pure diamond dazzle. Fancy yellow radiant cut diamond set in platinum." We, too, have a faith that dazzles.

When you feel as if your faith is weak, and you are struggling to keep your head above water in a spiritual sense, remember these six truths about your faith jewel. They will encourage you to keep your hope fresh and vibrant in the darkest of storms and during the easiest of times.

God sees your faith. Jesus said to the believers at Thyatira, "I know all the things you do—your love, your faith, your service, and your patient endurance. And I can see your constant improvement in all these things" (Rev. 2:19). He sees your faith too. He is your greatest advocate, your most ardent cheerleader. He sends His Holy Spirit to bolster your faith and to give you hope when things seem hopeless. He will also remind you to keep true to your faith when you are tempted to ease up when times are good. None of the faith you build in your life will go unnoticed by Him.

Your faith is precious to God. Have you ever watched a movie in which an adventurer finds a cave full of jewels piled high to the ceiling? Do you ever imagine that God's riches are so immense that He has palaces full of precious gems? If He is so rich, then perhaps He doesn't consider what you have to be valuable. Not so. First Peter 1:7 says, "Your faith is far more precious to God than mere gold." Isn't it wonderful, when you sometimes feel insecure or worthless, to know how valuable God considers your faith?

Your faith is made complete by your actions. If you find that your faith is wavering or you are getting discouraged, take hope. God doesn't expect you to have a fully matured faith right now. He is building that into your life. James writes about Abraham, "You see, he was trusting God so much that he was willing to do whatever God told him to do. His faith was made complete by what he did—by his actions" (Jas. 2:22). When you waver, just obey God. Your actions will build your faith and your faith will build your actions. They work together.

We can fully trust God. Have you ever felt like you are so insignificant that you should cower in front of God? Or that you could never be worth enough to have a direct conversation with Him? Hebrews 10:22 tells us, "Let us go right into the presence of God, with true hearts fully trusting him. For our evil consciences have been sprinkled with Christ's blood to make us clean, and our bodies have been washed with pure water." This means that Christ has paid for our sins, so our faith in Him has made us worthy to come before God!

Faith will protect us. Did you know that God assures us that our faith will protect us from the attacks of our enemies? Paul writes, "Let us who live in the light think clearly, protected by the body armor of faith and love, and wearing as our helmet the confidence of our salvation" (1 Thess. 5:8). I know this is true. I have seen nonbelievers lured into doing many harmful activities because they have no foundation of faith. How many times I have thanked God that He has given me His protection of wisdom and strength that keeps me safe from things that would harm me!

We are encouraged by the faith of each other. Romans 1:12 says, "I'm eager to encourage you in your faith, but I also want to be encouraged by yours. In this way, each of us will be a blessing to each other." How many times has this happened to you? You stop to have a visit with a friend, and she tells you how God is working in her life. You come away from the visit with your heart full of encouragement after hearing her story. And I'm sure you have built up someone else when you shared your faith moments. This is one of the privileges of being part of God's family.

Use these six points to keep your faith strong. Keep your goal of faith in mind at all times. I want you to imagine what you will experience when you realize your faith. What will that moment be like when you first step into the presence of Jesus? This is the time when Hebrews 11:1 will be fulfilled in your life: "What is faith? It is the confident assurance that what we hope for is going to happen. It is the evidence of things we cannot yet see." What we cannot see right now but what we are truly assured will happen will be proven fact when we see Jesus.

The apostle John was given a vision of what we will see in heaven. He writes in Revelation 4:2-6:

> I saw a throne in heaven and someone sitting on it! The one sitting on the throne was as brilliant as gemstones—jasper and carnelian. And the glow of an emerald circled his throne like a rainbow. Twenty-four thrones surrounded him, and twenty-four elders sat on them. They were all clothed in white and had gold crowns on their heads. And from the throne came flashes of lightning and the rumble of thunder. And in front of the throne were seven lampstands with burning flames. They are the seven spirits of God. In front of the throne was a shiny sea of glass, sparkling like crystal.

In heaven, we will also see and hear millions of angels singing praises to the Lamb of God, Jesus Christ. They will sing, "The Lamb is worthy—the Lamb who was killed. He is worthy to receive power and riches and wisdom and strength and honor and glory and blessing" (Rev. 5:12). Then everyone, including you and me, will join in on the praises. We will sing, "Blessing and honor and glory and power belong to the one sitting on the throne and to the Lamb forever and ever" (v. 13).

This will be just the beginning of an eternity of enjoying the presence of our Lord and Savior. It will be an adventure more fulfilling and wonderful than anything we can imagine now. No longer will we battle against temptation and sin. Illness and fatigue will be in the past. Sadness and death will be just a memory. We will be reunited with those who have gone on before us.

It's so true. Your faith is a gem worth more than the most expensive diamond in the world. And you can never lose your jewel. It is hidden in your heart, nestled securely in the Holy Spirit's care. Its sparkle shines out most clearly during those moments of faith when you see what God is doing in your life through faith. So, put on your diamond ring of faith and tell the world what Jesus means to you! And keep the hope. You will soon see the object of your love—our Lord Jesus, radiant and glorious!

May the reality of an authentic faith be yours!

A Pathway to Deepen My Faith

1. Learning from the Chapter
Paraphrase Revelation 2:19 to help you explain what you hope to do with your faith.

_____

_____

_____

_____

_____

Read Hebrews 11:1. This is the central verse of the book. Now that you have learned more about faith and how to apply it in your life, what does it mean to you now that it didn't mean before? How has your understanding of faith changed?

_____

_____

_____

_____

_____

_____

2. Knowing God's Word

The following points are the six truths about your faith. Read each point and the accompanying verse, and then explain what each point means to your faith in Christ.

1. God sees your faith—Revelation 2:19

_____

_____

_____

_____

_____

2. Your faith is precious to God—1 Peter 1:7

_____

_____

_____

_____

_____

3. Your faith is made complete by your actions—James 2:22

_____

_____

_____

_____

4. We can fully trust God—Hebrews 10:22

_____

_____

_____

_____

_____

_____

5. Faith will protect us—1 Thessalonians 5:8

_____

_____

_____

_____

_____

_____

6. We are encouraged by the faith of each other—Romans 1:12

_____

_____

_____

_____

_____

3. Applying God's Word
Review each of the six truths and the corresponding verses and explain how you are going to use each point to build your faith.

_____

_____

_____

_____

_____

_____

Read Revelation 4:2-6. How does the scene described in these verses in Revelation help you stay assured of your faith when times are difficult?

_____

_____

_____

_____

_____

_____

_____

As I explained, Bill's death was one of the most difficult yet glorious faith moments of my life. Do you have an event in your life that you could say the same? How will you go on building your faith, using Hebrews 11:1 as a comfort and hope?

_____

_____

_____

_____

_____

_____

_____

Now turn to Revelation 5:12-13. Use these verses to thank Jesus for your faith, and praise Him for what He has done for you.

_____

_____

_____

_____

_____

_____

_____

Ask God to help you build your faith through faith moments that will glorify Him and lead others to faith in Christ.

Beginning Your Journey of Joy

These Four Principles Are Essential in Beginning a Journey of Joy.

One—*God loves you and created you to know Him personally.*

God's Love

"God so loved the world that He gave His one and only Son, that whoever believes in Him shall not perish but have eternal life" (John 3:16).

God's Plan

"Now this is eternal life: that they may know you, the only true God, and Jesus Christ, whom you have sent" (John 17:3).

What prevents us from knowing God personally?

Two—*People are sinful and separated from God, so we cannot know Him personally or experience His love.*

People Are Sinful

"All have sinned and fall short of the glory of God" (Romans 3:23).

People were created to have fellowship with God; but, because of our own stubborn self-will, we chose to go our own independent way and fellowship with God was broken. This self-will, characterized by an attitude of active rebellion or passive indifference, is an evidence of what the Bible calls sin.

People Are Separated

"The wages of sin is death" [spiritual separation from God] (Romans 6:23).

This diagram illustrates that God is holy and people are sinful. A great gulf separates the two. The arrows illustrate that people are continually trying to reach God and establish a personal relationship with Him through our own efforts, such as a good life, philosophy, or religion—but we inevitably fail.

The third principle explains the only way to bridge this gulf . . .

Three—*Jesus Christ is God's only provision for our sin. Through Him alone we can know God personally and experience His love.*

He Died in Our Place

"God demonstrates His own love toward us, in that while we were yet sinners, Christ died for us" (Romans 5:8).

He Rose from the Dead

"Christ died for our sins . . . He was buried . . . He was raised on the third day according to the Scriptures . . . He appeared to Peter, then to the twelve. After that He appeared to more than five hundred . . ." (1 Corinthians 15:3-6).

He Is the Only Way to God

"Jesus said to him, 'I am the way, and the truth, and the life; no one comes to the Father but through Me'" (John 14:6).

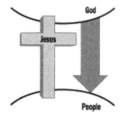

This diagram illustrates that God has bridged the gulf that separates us from Him by sending His Son, Jesus Christ, to die on the cross in our place to pay the penalty for our sins.

It is not enough just to know these three truths . . .

Four—We must individually receive Jesus Christ as Savior and Lord; then we can know God personally and experience His love.

We Must Receive Christ
"As many as received Him, to them He gave the right to become children of God, even to those who believe in His name" (John 1:12).

We Receive Christ Through Faith
"By grace you have been saved through faith; and that not of yourselves, it is the gift of God; not as a result of works that no one should boast" (Ephesians 2:8,9).

When We Receive Christ, We Experience a New Birth
(Read John 3:1–8.)

We Receive Christ by Personal Invitation
[Christ speaking] "Behold, I stand at the door and knock; if anyone hears My voice and opens the door, I will come in to him" (Revelation 3:20).

Receiving Christ involves turning to God from self (repentance) and trusting Christ to come into our lives to forgive us of our sins and to make us what He wants us to be. Just to agree intellectually that Jesus Christ is the Son of God and that He died on the cross for our sins is not enough. Nor is it enough to have an emotional experience. We receive Jesus Christ by faith, as an act of our will.

These two circles represent two kinds of lives:

Self-Directed Life
S – Self is on the throne
† – Christ is outside the life
● – Interests are directed by self, often resulting in discord and frustration

Christ-Directed Life
† – Christ is in the life and on the throne
S – Self is yielding to Christ
● – Interests are directed by Christ, resulting in harmony with God's plan

Which circle best represents your life?
Which circle would you like to have represent your life?

The following explains how you can receive Christ:

You Can Receive Christ Right Now
by Faith Through Prayer
(Prayer is talking with God)

God knows your heart and is not so concerned with your words as He is with the attitude of your heart. The following is a suggested prayer:

Lord Jesus, I want to know You personally. Thank You for dying on the cross for my sins. I open the door of my life and receive You as my Savior and Lord. Thank You for forgiving my sins and giving me eternal life. Take control of the throne of my life. Make me the kind of person You want me to be.

Does this prayer express the desire of your heart?

If it does, I invite you to pray this prayer right now, and Christ will come into your life, as He promised.

How to Know That Christ Is in Your Life

Did you receive Christ into your life? According to His promise in Revelation 3:20, where is Christ right now in relation to you? Christ said that He would come into your life. Would He mislead you? On what authority do you know that God has answered your prayer? (The trustworthiness of God Himself and His Word.)

The Bible Promises Eternal Life to All Who Receive Christ

"The witness is this, that God has given us eternal life, and this life is in His Son. He who has the Son has the life; he who does not have the Son of God does not have the life. These things I have written to you who believe in the name of the Son of God, in order that you may know that you have eternal life" (1 John 5:11–13).

Thank God often that Christ is in your life and that He will never leave you (Hebrews 13:5). You can know on the basis of His promise that Christ lives in you and that you have eternal life from the very moment you invite Him in. He will not deceive you.

An important reminder . . .

Feelings Can Be Unreliable
You might have expectations about how you should feel after placing your trust in Christ. While feelings are important, they are unreliable indicators of your sincerity or the trustworthiness of God's promise. Our feelings change easily, but God's Word and His character remain constant. This illustration shows the relationship among *fact* (God and His Word), *faith* (our trust in God and His Word), and our *feelings*.

Fact: The chair is strong enough to support you.
Faith: You believe this chair will support you, so you sit in it.
Feeling: You may or may not feel comfortable in this chair, but it continues to support you.

The promise of God's Word, the Bible—not our feelings—is our authority. The Christian lives by faith (trust) in the trustworthiness of God Himself and His Word.

Now That You Have Entered Into a Personal Relationship With Christ
The moment you received Christ by faith, as an act of your will, many things happened, including the following:

1. Christ came into your life (Revelation 3:20; Colossians 1:27).
2. Your sins were forgiven (Colossians 1:14).
3. You became a child of God (John 1:12).
4. You received eternal life (John 5:24).
5. You began the great adventure for which God created you (John 10:10; 2 Corinthians 5:17; 1 Thessalonians 5:18).

Can you think of anything more wonderful that could happen to you than entering into a personal relationship with Jesus Christ? Would you like to thank God in prayer right now for what He has done for you? By thanking God, you demonstrate your faith.

To enjoy your new relationship with God...

Suggestions for Christian Growth
Spiritual growth results from trusting Jesus Christ. "The righteous man shall live by faith" (Galatians 3:11). A life of faith will enable you to trust God increasingly with every detail of your life, and to practice the following:

G *Go* to God in prayer daily (John 15:7).

R *Read* God's Word daily (Acts 17:11); begin with the Gospel of John.

O *Obey* God moment by moment (John 14:21).

W *Witness* for Christ by your life and words (Matthew 4:19; John 15:8).

T *Trust* God for every detail of your life (1 Peter 5:7).

H *Holy Spirit*—allow Him to control and empower your daily life and witness (Galatians 5:16,17; Acts 1:8; Ephesians 5:18).

Fellowship in a Good Church

God's Word admonishes us not to forsake "the assembling of ourselves together" (Hebrews 10:25). Several logs burn brightly together, but put one aside on the cold hearth and the fire goes out. So it is with your relationship with other Christians. If you do not belong to a church, do not wait to be invited. Take the initiative; call the pastor of a nearby church where Christ is honored and His Word is preached. Start this week, and make plans to attend regularly.

Adapted from *The Four Spiritual Laws*, written by Bill Bright. © Campus Crusade for Christ International, Orlando, Florida.

Satisfied?

Satisfaction: (n.) fulfillment of one's needs, longings, or desires

What words would you use to describe your current experience as a Christian?

Growing	Painful	Empty
Disappointing	Guilty	Duty
Forgiven	So-so	Mediocre
Struggling	Frustrated	Dynamic
Defeated	Fulfilled	Vital
Up and down	Stuck	Others?
Discouraged	Joyful	
Intimate	Exciting	

Do you desire more? Jesus said, "If anyone is thirsty, let him come to me and drink. Whoever believes in me, as the Scripture has said, streams of living water will flow from within him" (John 7:37,38).

What did Jesus mean? John, the biblical author, went on to explain, "By this he meant the Spirit, whom those who believed in him were later to receive. Up to that time the Spirit had not been given, since Jesus had not yet been glorified" (John 7:39).

Jesus promised that God's Holy Spirit would satisfy the thirst, or deepest longings, of all who believe in Jesus Christ. However, many Christians do not understand the Holy Spirit or how to experience Him in their daily lives.

The following principles will help you understand and enjoy God's Spirit.

The Divine Gift
Divine: (adj.) given by God

God has given us His Spirit so that we can experience intimacy with Him and enjoy all He has for us.

The Holy Spirit is the source of our deepest satisfaction.

The Holy Spirit is God's permanent presence with us.

"Jesus said, 'I will ask the Father, and he will give you another Counselor to be with you forever—the Spirit of truth'" (John 14:16,17).

The Holy Spirit enables us to understand and experience all God has given us.

We have not received the spirit of the world but the Spirit who is from God, that we may understand what God has freely given us (1 Corinthians 2:12).

The Holy Spirit enables us to experience many things:

- A genuine new spiritual life (John 3:1–8).
- The assurance of being a child of God (Romans 8:15,16).
- The infinite love of God (Romans 5:5; Ephesians 3:18,19).

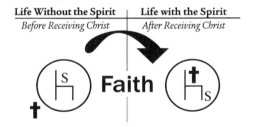

"The man without the Spirit does not accept the things that come from the Spirit of God, for they are foolishness to him, and he cannot understand them, because they are spiritually discerned" (1 Corinthians 2:14).

"The spiritual man makes judgments about all things. . . . We have the mind of Christ" (1 Corinthians 2:15,16).

"But those who are controlled by the Holy Spirit think about things that please the Spirit" (Romans 8:5, *NLT*).

Why are many Christians not satisfied in their experience with God?

The Present Danger
Danger: (n.) a thing that may cause injury, loss, or pain

We cannot experience intimacy with God and enjoy all He has for us if we fail to depend on His Spirit.

People who trust in their own efforts and strength to live the Christian life will experience failure and frustration, as will those who live to please themselves rather than God.

We cannot live the Christian life in our own strength.

> "Are you so foolish? After beginning with the Spirit, are you now trying to attain your goal by human effort?" (Galatians 3:3).

We cannot enjoy all God desires for us if we live by our self-centered desires.

> "For the sinful nature desires what is contrary to the Spirit, and the Spirit what is contrary to the sinful nature. They are in conflict with each other, so that you do not do what you want" (Galatians 5:17).

Three Kinds of Lifestyles

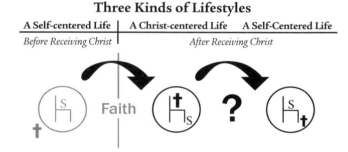

A Self-centered Life	A Christ-centered Life	A Self-Centered Life
Before Receiving Christ	*After Receiving Christ*	

> "Brothers, I could not address you as spiritual, but as worldly—mere infants in Christ. I gave you milk, not solid food, for you were not yet ready for it. Indeed, you are still not ready. You are still worldly. For since there is jealousy and quarreling among you, are you not worldly? Are you not acting like mere men?" (1 Corinthians 3:1-3).

How can we develop a lifestyle of depending on the Spirit?

The Intimate Journey
Journey: (n.) any course from one experience to another

By walking in the Spirit we increasingly experience intimacy with God and enjoy all He has for us.

Walking in the Spirit moment by moment is a lifestyle. It is learning to depend upon the Holy Spirit for His abundant resources as a way of life.

As we walk in the Spirit, we have the ability to live a life pleasing to God.

"So I say, live by the Spirit, and you will not gratify the desires of the sinful nature. . . . Since we live by the Spirit, let us keep in step with the Spirit" (Galatians 5:16,25).

As we walk in the Spirit, we experience intimacy with God and all He has for us.

"But the fruit of the Spirit is love, joy, peace, patience, kindness, goodness, faithfulness, gentleness and self-control" (Galatians 5:22,23).

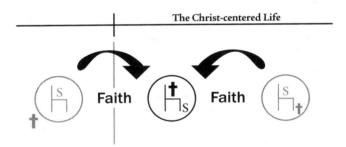

Faith (trust in God and His promises) is the only way a Christian can live by the Spirit.

Spiritual breathing is a powerful word picture which can help you experience moment-by-moment dependence upon the Spirit.

Exhale: Confess your sin the moment you become aware of it—agree with God concerning it and thank Him for His forgiveness, according to 1 John 1:9 and Hebrews 10:1-25. Confession requires repentance—a change in attitude and action.

Inhale: Surrender control of your life to Christ, and rely upon the Holy Spirit to fill you with His presence and power by faith, according to His command (Ephesians 5:18) and promise (1 John 5:14,15).

How does the Holy Spirit fill us with His power?

The Empowering Presence
Empower: (v.) to give ability to

We are filled with the Spirit by faith, enabling us to experience intimacy with God and enjoy all He has for us.

The essence of the Christian life is what God does in and through us, not what we do for God. Christ's life is reproduced in the believer by the power of the Holy Spirit. To be filled with the Spirit is to be directed and empowered by Him.

By faith, we experience God's power through the Holy Spirit.

"I pray that out of his glorious riches he may strengthen you with power through his Spirit in your inner being, so that Christ may dwell in your hearts through faith" (Ephesians 3:16,17).

Three important questions to ask yourself:

1. Am I ready now to surrender control of my life to our Lord Jesus Christ? (Romans 12:1,2).

2. Am I ready now to confess my sins? (1 John 1:9). Sin grieves God's Spirit (Ephesians 4:30). But God in His love has for-

given all of your sins—past, present, and future—because Christ has died for you.

3. Do I sincerely desire to be directed and empowered by the Holy Spirit? (John 7:37–39).

By faith claim the fullness of the Spirit according to His command and promise:

God COMMANDS us to be filled with the Spirit.

". . . Be filled with the Spirit" (Ephesians 5:18).

God PROMISES He will always answer when we pray according to His will.

"This is the confidence we have in approaching God: that if we ask anything according to his will, he hears us. And if we know that he hears us—whatever we ask—we know that we have what we asked of him" (1 John 5:14,15).

How to pray to be filled with the Holy Spirit . . .

The Turning Point
Turning point: time when a decisive change occurs

We are filled with the Holy Spirit by faith alone.

Sincere prayer is one way of expressing our faith. The following is a suggested prayer:

Dear Father, I need You. I acknowledge that I have sinned against You by directing my own life. I thank You that You have forgiven my sins through Christ's death on the cross for me. I now invite Christ to again take His place on the throne of my life. Fill me with the Holy Spirit as You commanded me to be filled, and as You promised in Your Word that You would do if I asked in faith. I pray

this in the name of Jesus. I now thank You for filling me with the
Holy Spirit and directing my life.

Does this prayer express the desire of your heart? If so, you can
pray right now and trust God to fill you with His Holy Spirit.
How to know that you are filled by the Holy Spirit:

- Did you ask God to fill you with the Holy Spirit?
- Do you know that you are now filled with the Holy Spirit?
- On what authority? (On the trustworthiness of God
  Himself and His Word: Hebrews 11:6; Romans 14:22,23.)

As you continue to depend on God's Spirit moment by moment you will experience and enjoy intimacy with God and all He
has for you—a truly rich and satisfying life.

An important reminder . . .

Do Not Depend on Feelings
The promise of God's Word, the Bible—not our feelings—is our authority. The Christian lives by faith (trust) in the trustworthiness
of God Himself and His Word. Flying in an airplane can illustrate
the relationship among fact (God and His Word), faith (our trust
in God and His Word), and feeling (the result of our faith and obedience) (John 14:21).

To be transported by an airplane, we must place our faith in the
trustworthiness of the aircraft and the pilot who flies it. Our feelings of confidence or fear do not affect the ability of the airplane

to transport us, though they do affect how much we enjoy the trip. In the same way, we as Christians do not depend on feelings or emotions, but we place our faith (trust) in the trustworthiness of God and the promises of His Word.

Now That You Are Filled with the Holy Spirit

Thank God that the Spirit will enable you:

- To glorify Christ with your life (John 16:14).
- To grow in your understanding of God and His Word (1 Corinthians 2:14,15).
- To live a life pleasing to God (Galatians 5:16-23).

Remember the promise of Jesus:

"But you will receive power when the Holy Spirit comes on you; and you will be my witnesses in Jerusalem, and in all Judea and Samaria, and to the ends of the earth" (Acts 1:8).

If you would like additional resources on the Holy Spirit, please go to **www.nlpdirect.com**.

Adapted from *Have You Made the Wonderful Discovery of the Spirit-filled Life?* Written by Bill Bright, © 1966, 1995 Campus Crusade for Christ International, Orlando, Florida.

ACKNOWLEDGMENTS

I owe a great debt of gratitude to Dr. Henrietta Mears. She led me to Christ by explaining for the first time, to my understanding, what it is to believe by faith.

I was engaged to be married to Bill Bright. He was growing in his faith as he was taught by Dr. Henrietta Mears and Dr. Louis Evans at Hollywood Presbyterian Church. I was a professing Christian and had been a leader in the youth group of my denomination. Bill had proposed to me because he thought I was a Christian. I had the right words and standards.

In the summer of 1947, Bill had an encounter with the Holy Spirit that was life-changing. He tried to explain this in letters to me. I interpreted this incident as his being led by a group of influential people. Bill and I realized we were not united in our faith, and this would have to be resolved before we could commit to marriage. After graduation from college, I went to California to rescue him from these people. The result, of course, was that I was the one rescued.

The people I met were beautiful, radiant, successful, enthusiastic and talked freely about their faith. I had never met people like this. Though I was impressed, I concluded that they were new in their faith and soon would get back to normal.

Bill asked if I would go talk with Miss Mears, "teacher," as many called her. She met me with open arms. We sat in comfortable chairs across from each other, with her Bible in hand. She began to explain how God loved me. He did not want me to live a "hum-drum" existence, but a life of meaning and purpose. She explained, verse by verse, basically what Bill developed as the *Four Spiritual Laws*.

Miss Mears, as a former chemistry teacher, explained that just as we go into a chemistry laboratory to perform an experiment following the table of chemical valence, and we can expect a certain reaction, so too can we go into "God's laboratory" and follow His laws and also expect the results He promises.

I shared with her that I had prayed to receive Christ many times. Every time an invitation was given in church, I went forward to receive Christ or to rededicate my life. My resolve worked for about three days and then I was back to being the same old person, with temper, unresolved conflicts, trying hard to love people and be happy. It did not show from the outside, and I thought I was really living a pretty good life.

Miss Mears challenged me with, "If God is real, Jesus Christ is the way you get to know God," and promised me a more abundant life. Wouldn't I be foolish not to know Him as my personal Savior?

I had to agree. She challenged me again with the thought that I had nothing to lose if He did not prove Himself, but everything to gain if He did. I consented to pray one last time to ask Him to enter my life. I was so afraid it would not be different, but it was! John 1:12 became real to me:

> But to as many as did receive *and* welcome Him, He gave the authority (power, privilege, right) to become the children of God, that is, to those who believe in (adhere to, trust in, and rely on) His name (*AMP*).

After four years of marriage, circumstances made it convenient for Henrietta, Bill and me to combine households. She was mature enough to be patient with our (my) immaturity, and we were young enough to adjust to her needs. I learned through Miss Mears and Bill to trust God with everything. I learned the practicality of the Spirit-filled life and to apply Scripture in every circumstance. Eventually, I learned "to believe God for the impossible."

I had mentioned to Miss Mears that when we had children, it would be necessary for us to move. She firmly assured me that her home would be a wonderful place to rear children. She taught me that children can learn boundaries and that they can learn to appreciate the lovely, breakable items that she had in abundance.

Our first child, Zac, was born less than a year after we combined households. Henrietta could not have been more enthusiastic. She "cooed and gooed" with him, prayed over him and loved

him, as she did all children. One afternoon when Zac was about
three weeks old, she volunteered to babysit for us. He cried much
of the time, though she found playing music on the radio kept
him a little more satisfied. She never offered to babysit again.

Miss Mears had spent most of her life writing Sunday School
materials for all ages, but her love for small children was very evident. Zac attended his first conference at Indian Village at Forest Home at the age of eight. We had "no no" lines to define
spaces where children could not go. When Brad was born a few
years later, Miss Mears found both boys a delight.

We moved to Arrowhead Springs before Brad's fifth birth-
day. The only thing that had not worked out perfectly in our
moving to Arrowhead Springs was someone to live with Henrietta. God brought someone to mind, and Louise James moved
in with Miss Mears.

God called our dear friend to her heavenly home in March
1963. The impact she made on our lives most certainly has eternal significance. I feel certain that I would not be able to take advantage of many of the opportunities I have had, or have even
now, had I not learned so much of faith and ministry from Henrietta Mears.

I also owe a debt of gratitude to Brenda Josee, who has been
tenacious in encouraging me to write in the past, but has particularly been after me to write this book of faith. Thank you, Brenda.
I love and appreciate you.

When Bill Greig III, of Gospel Light Publications, asked to
publish this manuscript, I was highly complimented, and I appreciate the love and admiration we share in our connection with
Henrietta Mears—she as his relative and the founder of Gospel
Light Press; and as my friend and mentor. I so appreciate the work
of the staff of Gospel Light in helping this book become a reality.
Again, to God be the glory!